Advance Praise for

<u>Moving to Mexico's Lake Chapala</u>

"I found it highly readable, most comprehensive, and flawlessly organized. I think it's the best book of its kind that I have read, and I have been down here for 25 years."
          Alejandro Grattan-Dominguez
          Editor-in-Chief, El Ojo del Lago Magazine

"I've lived at Lakeside for ten years now, and coordinate the Information Desk at the Lake Chapala Society. Yet I'm amazed at how much I learned reading this book. I fully intend to keep a copy at the Information Desk, and suggest all the volunteers familiarize themselves with it."
          Harriet Hart
          Lakeside writer

"I thoroughly enjoyed the read. I wish I had your book available when I moved here 8 years ago. It certainly would have made life simpler and more interesting."
          Howard Feldstein
          President, Lake Chapala Society

"A valuable resource for anyone visiting or moving to Lake Chapala. If you can, buy it before you come. At the very least, buy it the moment you arrive. Having this book when I moved here 11 years ago would have saved me many missteps and countless hours of research."
          Judy Dykstra-Brown
          Lakeside writer and artist

Moving to Mexico's Lake Chapala

Checklists, How-To's, and Practical Information and Advice for Expats and Retirees

Fourth Edition

Lisa L. Jorgensen
Mexico Expat Press
Ajijic, Jalisco, México

www.LakeChapalaReporter.com
info@LakeChapalaReporter.com

Fourth Edition

Copyright © 2017 by Lisa L. Jorgensen

All international rights reserved. No part of this book may be reproduced in any form by any means, electrical or mechanical, including photocopying, recording, storing in any information retrieval system, or transmitting without prior written permission from the copyright holder. Reviewers may quote brief extracts in a review.

The information presented in this guide is the most current as of the published date. It is not intended to replace legal or medical professionals' counsel. The publisher and author disclaim any liability to any party for any loss or damage caused by errors, omissions, or any disruption of plans, events, or outcomes.

Neither the author nor the publisher receives any personal, commercial, financial, or in-kind consideration from any merchants or services presented herein.

ISBN: 978-0-9859476-4-4

Mexico Expat Press
Ajijic, Jalisco, Mexico

To submit corrections or additions to the next edition, email: info@LakeChapalaReporter.com

Table of Contents

Introduction to the Fourth Edition 5
Introduction to the Third Edition 6
Introduction to the Second Edition 8
Introduction to the First Edition 9

Part 1
Your Exploratory Trip..13
Chapter 1
Planning Your Trip 14
Chapter 2
During Your Trip 21

Part 2
Before Your Move..33
Chapter 1
Consider Your Finances...34
Chapter 2
Choosing Your Move Date 38
Chapter 3
Telling Your Family and Friends............................39
Chapter 4
What About Your Pets? 41
Chapter 5
What About Your House?.......................................44
Chapter 6
What About Your Car? 47
Chapter 7
What About Your Other Belongings?....................52
Chapter 8
Four Weeks Before Moving....................................65
Chapter 9
Three Weeks Before Moving..................................73
Chapter 10
Two Weeks Before Moving 78
Chapter 11
One Week Before Moving 82

Part 3
Your Move 85
Chapter 1
Driving to the Border 86
Chapter 2
At the Mexican Border..90
Chapter 3
Driving to Lake Chapala 100

Part 4
Your First Few Weeks at Lake Chapala......................103
Chapter 1
Your First Week..104
Chapter 2
Your Second Week 114
Chapter 3
Your Third Week 116
Chapter 4
Whenever You Can..119

Part 5
Living at Lake Chapala 123
Chapter 1
Legal Basics..126
Chapter 2
The Towns 130
Chapter 3
Language and Social Customs 139
Chapter 4
Getting Around 149
Chapter 5
Shopping 170
Chapter 6
Crime and Safety..193

Table of Contents

Part 5 (continued)
Living at Lake Chapala

Chapter 7
Medical Care 196
Chapter 8
Home Life and Services 209
Chapter 9
Utilities 220
Chapter 10
Technology 225
Chapter 11
Banking 236
Chapter 12
Government Services 240

Appendix 259

Exploratory Trip Checklist 259
Move Planning Checklist 260
Border Checklist 263
Moving In Checklist 264
Recommended Reading 266
Places and Services 268
Vehicle Accident Form 270
Common Conversions 277
Telephone Dialing 279
Emergency Numbers and Words 281

Index 283

Introduction (Fourth Edition)

Over two years have passed since the Third Edition was published. There have been no very significant changes during this time, which accounts for the delay. The minimum wage rate has changed, however, which is the basis for many Mexican government fees, such as immigration visa fees and traffic penalties. So, those have been updated in this edition.

All other changes have been made simply to further clarify concepts or procedures.

I am still the publisher and editor of the online magazine **The Lake Chapala Reporter**, which serves as an extension of this book. It contains five years of articles, how-to's, and updated information for everyone fortunate enough to live in and visit the Lake Chapala area.

                    Lisa L. Jorgensen
                    Ajijic, Jalisco, México
                    September 2017
                    info@LakeChapalaReporter.com

Introduction (Third Edition)

Each new year, it seems, brings significant changes to the life of expats at Lake Chapala. Hence, the need for yet another edition of this book. There were two important changes during this last year.

The first change was the exposure of widespread sales commission price fixing (guilty verdicts and 28 million pesos in fines) by most of the local real estate brokers and owners (those who were members of the local multiple listing service (MLS)) between the years 2003 and 2008. The sales commission rates have not changed in the interim, leading to speculation that the price fixing continues. I therefore recommend employing only the services of independent real estate brokers and agents. This is covered in Part 1, Chapter 2, which is about activities related to exploratory trips to this area. The issue is addressed there because many people buy property prior to moving here, and hence, before really understanding the real estate market.

The second change was the reduction of financial requirements to qualify for residential visas. The immigration law of 2012 set the financial requirements significantly higher than previously, and had a dampening effect on immigration (and therefore business) in 2013 and 2014. The requirements were lowered in late 2014 to rates more consistent with what typical retirees can afford.

Introduction (Third Edition)

There were many smaller changes, as well, including a new telecommunications law eliminating long distance charges for calls within Mexico. The primary telephone service carrier, TelMex, even eliminated long distance charges internationally, in some cases.

And, of course, I made the usual editorial changes I cannot resist making—shortening sentences, clarifying concepts, and correcting comma misdeeds.

I still write for and edit the online magazine **The Lake Chapala Reporter**, which serves as an extension of this book. It contains further how-tos, and updated information for all expats living in this beautiful and bountiful Lake Chapala area.

                    Lisa L. Jorgensen
                    Ajijic, Jalisco, México
                    April 2015
                    info@LakeChapalaReporter.com

Introduction (Second Edition)

It's been a year and a half since I wrote the first introduction. The biggest change since then has been the overhaul of the Mexican immigration system, increasing the financial requirements for immigrants to obtain residence visas, requiring first-time visa applications to be started at home-country Mexican consulates, and limiting temporary visas to four years. These changes urged me to establish a web site (**LakeChapalaReporter.com**) so readers can stay abreast of not only the changes, but the implications of the changes and how they are being interpreted and implemented by various immigration offices. The web site started out small, but has since grown into an online magazine (without local advertisements, so it can stay impartial), encompassing not only immigration issues, but all the issues covered in this book and beyond. Any updates to this edition of the book will also be posted there.

On a personal note: yes, I still live here, and I still love it here. There's nothing in my first introduction that I would change. But now, in addition to what I wrote about my first impressions, it's a pleasure to meet people who kindly mention to me that the book has been helpful to them. I hope it will be to you, too.

Lisa L. Jorgensen
Ajijic, Jalisco, Mexico
March 2014

Introduction (First Edition)

I've been watching the avocado dangling over my head as I write in my back yard. Having only seen avocados in supermarkets in the US, I didn't know how long this one would take to ripen—whether it would be ready before this book was. But it has kept up with me quite well, rounding out at about the same rate as this book.

A year ago, I could not have imagined that I would be sitting under an avocado tree in Mexico, living this new life. After building a full corporate career in the US, and spending a few years owning and operating an international online retail business on the East Coast, I decided the time had come for me to retire. I was burned out on 7-day-a-week, 10-hour days on the computer, and I was barely making a profit during the recession. My quality of life was flat, and I was in a rut. In other words, I needed to find a new way to live. After making a list of my priorities and criteria, I spent some time doing research on the Internet, looking for the best places in the world to retire comfortably on my Social Security retirement benefits. That place turned out to be the Lake Chapala area in the state of Jalisco in Mexico.

Life for me has become a wonder, one that I would wish upon you, too, if you're ready. You don't have to be ready to retire, necessarily. You just have to be ready for a richer life. Many other people have already decided that they were ready, with over 7,000 expats (up to 15,000 in the winter) now living in the Lake Chapala area. And, many retirement guides are claiming that Lake Chapala is better than Florida for retiring baby boomers because it's less expensive (you can live well on $1,200 per month per person here), it's less humid, it's culturally rich, and the health care is excellent. Most of us are from the US and Canada. Some have come as "snowbirds," escaping cold weather in winter. Others have come as "sunbirds," escaping hot and humid weather in summer. And some, like me, have come as "lifebirds"—here to stay.

What do we do all day? The expatriate community is quite social. Some play bridge several times a week, some go to the hot springs, some play golf on beautiful green courses, some volunteer at animal shelters. Some go to the library and meet people in the parks and plazas. We even have theater groups to get involved in. But, of course, you can do those things north of the border, too. What we really do is experience life differently.

We go to the bustling open markets in the same way that our Mexican neighbors have for hundreds of years. We watch *folklórico* dancers spin and smile in their vivid striped skirts, just as they've also done for hundreds of years. Guadalajara, Mexico's second largest city, is less than an hour away, with its shopping, museums and culture, magnificent colonial architecture, nightlife, and sophistication. We watch children dance to the local mariachi bands their fathers play in. We learn their

Introduction (First Edition)

language and their customs, and get included in their large extended families. We get to experience a slower, more thoughtful pace of living (and cooking). Our minds free up so we can explore our artistic or literary sides. And, we get to experience the warm and generous natures of the Mexican people in a land full of surprises and deep beauty, in one of the best climates in the world.

I moved from the US to Lake Chapala in early 2012 with two dogs, two cats, and an SUV. This book was conceived during that trip out of my own need for information and advice. As most people do when they consider moving to a new country, I read the travel books about the region, as well as blogs and forums. But it became apparent that some important information was missing: advice on how to accomplish the move, and then practical knowledge of everyday living in this area, especially the sort of information I needed in the first month. For instance, I had questions about:

- Language – can I get along without knowing more Spanish than "Mi casa es su casa"? (Answer: yes)
- Driving – Should I take my car, or buy one there?
- Laws – Innocent until proven guilty? (Answer: not necessarily)
- Safety – Isn't it dangerous there? (Answer: no)
- Health and insurance – What options do I have? What about Medicare?
- Food and water – What's safe to eat and drink, and what isn't?

What I really needed was a helpful neighbor who knew how to plan for the move, and who knew the ins and outs of living here. So, that's how I hope you will come to think of this book—as a friendly neighbor close at hand with lots of useful information. The purpose is definitely not to ruin your joy of discovering things for yourself. You'll notice that there are no recommendations for restaurants, bed-and-breakfast hotels, hot spring spas, or points of interest. I leave that to the travel books, and to your own explorations and adventures.

Rather, while planning your move, and during the first few months when many important decisions need to be made, this practical day-to-day living guide is here to save you time, headaches, stomach aches, money—and even a night in the pokey for both you and your car.

The avocado over my head is ripe now, but I've also been watching a small bunch of green bananas lately, growing in the far corner of my yard. Life grows so abundantly here, even in the smallest of ways.

Lisa L. Jorgensen
Ajijic, Jalisco, México
August 2012

Part 1

Your Exploratory Trip

The best way to discover for yourself whether this life is right for you is to come to Lake Chapala for an exploratory trip. It will really be a vacation, but with a purpose: to determine whether the Lake Chapala area could be right for you for the long term. The time of year you choose doesn't really matter. It's almost always beautiful.

But, you will want to plan carefully so you'll get the most out of your stay, which the following chapters, together with the Exploratory Trip Checklist in the Appendix, will help you do most effectively.

Chapter 1

Planning Your Trip

The first step is for you to know what your needs and wants are, and to make a list of them. Do you need top quality schools for your children? Do you want to be in an area with arts and theatre? Do you want to be in an area with lots of other expats, or would you rather live in a more integrated way with traditional Mexican neighbors? How important are each of the criteria you choose? At the end of your trip, you can use your list to decide whether the Lake Chapala area will meet your needs, and which neighborhoods you'd like best. Put your concerns on your list, too. The list will be highly personal to you, of course, but I can tell you that for me, the three biggest concerns were:

1. Can I live reasonably well on my US Social Security retirement benefits alone? The answer was yes. A minimum of $1,500 per month for a single, or $2,000 for a couple is needed for a decent living in this area. This amount can come from some combination of dividends, interest, retirement, and social security benefits, or you can continue earning money through an Internet or consulting business—one that doesn't require you to be present in your home country very often. You can scrape by on less than the above amount, if you really need to (most Mexicans do, after all). There are still some rentals

Your Exploratory Trip: Planning Your Trip

here for $350 USD per month for the not-too discriminating. In general, the cost of living is 1/3 to ½ of what it is north of the border.

2. Will the quality and cost of health care meet my needs? The answer for me was yes. The quality of health care Lakeside is very good, and in Guadalajara, less than an hour away, health care is world class. The costs are much lower, including medications. And, Mexico also has universal health care (see Seguro Popular under Health Insurance in the Index).

3. Is it reasonably safe, even for a single woman? The answer, again, was yes. The narcotics cartels are not particularly interested in expat enclaves, and the Mexican government is very interested in protecting tourist and expat communities that pour millions of dollars into its economy without taking Mexican jobs. Non-drug-related crimes do exist, but they're comparatively low in number based on the size of the area, and they involve property crime much more than injury.

"In general, the cost of living is 1/3 to ½ of what it is north of the border."

Many people who choose to live here do so after having been here on vacation, or after getting tired of going back and forth year after year from their native country as snowbirds or sunbirds. But for those who've never been here, taking an exploratory trip (5 days or so) to the area is a very wise step, even if, like me, you're fairly certain it's going to be the right place for you. One reason is that it will help you solidify your decision. The second reason is that your move will be easier if you have a home to go to.

If you're planning to buy a home, there are many online resources that show you which homes are available, and how much they cost. Simply Google "Lake Chapala real estate." If you're planning to rent (which I recommend for the first 6 months), Google "Lake Chapala rentals." But you will also want to see what the different towns and neighborhoods are like in person. Your exploratory trip will be useful for that.

Incidentally, you will also notice that various tour packages are offered for prospective expats and retirees by some organizations. Be sure to research them carefully. Some are actually real estate groups that will monopolize your time while you are here. They will encourage you to purchase real estate, show you only their houses for sale, and make it difficult for you to make appointments with other real estate agencies, if you wish. I have talked with several people here who have had this complaint—and also that the tours seemed too expensive for what they were: captive sales tours. However, it may well be that not all tours are of this type.

Your Exploratory Trip: Planning Your Trip

If you are, indeed, interested in buying real estate in this area, I strongly encourage you to use only the services of an independent realty company. An independent realty company is one that does **_NOT_** belong to CAR (Chapala Association of Realtors) or GIL (*Grupo Immobiliario del Lago*), or the Chapala chapter of AMPI (*Asociación Mexicana de Profesionales Immobiliario*). The reason is that most of the members of those organizations were found guilty in Mexican federal court in 2015 of monopolistic price fixing between the years 2003 and 2008, and fined over 28 million pesos in penalties. (There were two appeals, which the realtors also lost.) They made illegal agreements among themselves to never charge less than 7% sales commission for residences or less than 10% for land. (Articles about this can be found on this book's companion website: LakeChapalaReporter.com). Despite the guilty verdicts and penalties, their commission rates have not changed much, leading to speculation that price fixing is still common. Independent realtors, by contrast, charge 5% sales commission for residences and 7% for land, which is also the norm in neighboring Guadalajara. The only two independent realty companies in the Lake Chapala area are Four Seasons Homes and All-in-1 Mexico. Of course, sales commissions are paid by sellers. But prospective buyers are

"The only two independent realty companies in the Lake Chapala area are Four Seasons Homes and All-in-1 Mexico."

17

also affected because the selling price is usually lower when working with independent realtors because they take less commission. The guilty realtors have made so much illegal money in the past off their fellow countrymen and women that it would be difficult to justify doing business with any of them. At the very least, prospective buyers should insist of fair commissions, namely 5% for residences and 7% for lots.

Until recently, all real estate in this area was sold on a cash basis. There are now some financing options available, but they do not have as favorable rates as north of the border. The down payments are much larger, and terms much shorter. So, do ask your prospective real estate agencies about their financing options, if that is an important consideration for you. You will probably be better off searching for funding north of the border first.

You'll want to make sure you have a valid passport that has more than 6 months before expiring. In fact, consider renewing your passport, regardless of how much time is left. Then you're good for 10 years, and won't be surprised later. Then, book a flight to the Guadalajara airport.

Your Exploratory Trip: Planning Your Trip

The best place to stay during your visit is at one of the many good bed and breakfast hotels (B&Bs) in the area. Just Google "Lake Chapala bed and breakfast." The reason B&Bs are ideal for your first trip is that you'll have ample opportunities to talk with the owners, who know the area well. They can help you in many ways: making suggestions, pointing you in the right direction, giving you important contact names, and answering many of your specific questions. You'll probably be meeting others just like yourself over breakfast, too, with whom you can compare notes and go out to dinner.

I highly recommend staying in the town of Ajijic for your first trip, since it's a central area for expats. When making your reservation, you'll want to ask for a first floor room if stairs are challenging for you. Also inquire about the noise in the area (roosters and bars).

> *"I highly recommend staying in the town of Ajijic for your first trip, since it's a central area for expats."*

You'll also want to ask whether they can reserve an enclosed overnight parking space for you if you plan to rent a car while you're here. On my exploratory trip, I rented a car for two of the days. I wanted to break free of my agency escort in order to get a flavor of other neighborhoods in the area, and to visit stores and some areas of interest. You won't need to make a decision about a rental car until you get here, though. Your days will be fluid. But when you do, be sure to read the section in this book regarding Rental Cars (check the Index).

And, don't forget to bring along the Exploratory Trip Checklist located in the Appendix.

Chapter 2

During Your Trip

Once you're at the Guadalajara Airport, it's not a good idea to just rent a car and drive to Lake Chapala by yourself on your first visit to the area. Unless you speak fluent Spanish, making sense of the signs to get out of the airport and onto the right highways and beyond would be too difficult. Either take a taxi from the airport, or ask your bed and breakfast (B&B) staff if they have a driver they can recommend who can pick you up at the airport and take you directly to the B&B. The trip will take about 30 to 45 minutes to Lake Chapala, and it will cost the equivalent of about $35 USD, plus you'll want to give the driver a 10 - 15% tip.

You'll need to pay for everything in pesos, which you can get at the best exchange rate at an airport ATM machine. The way to get a taxi at the airport, if you choose to do that, is to pay at the airport taxi counter, and then take your receipt outside to the *sitio* taxi stand. *Sitio* taxi drivers are licensed, registered, and insured, and are quite trustworthy. Many of them speak at least a little English. If you do take

"You'll need to pay for everything in pesos, which you can get at the best exchange rate at any ATM machine."

an airport taxi, ask your B&B to email you directions in English and Spanish, which you can give to the driver.

When you're here at Lake Chapala, you should have two base camps: the B&B where you're staying, and the (non-profit) Lake Chapala Society, which will most likely become like a second home to you. It's located in Ajijic at 16 de Septiembre #16-A where it meets Calle Corona (also called M. Castellanos). Aside from having beautiful grounds that will soothe your spirit, there's a whole world of information, activities, classes, community postings, health screenings, volunteer and charity opportunities, and expats like yourself there. If you decide to stay, you'll want to become a member to take advantage of everything they offer. The largest Mexican library of books in English is there, which, to me, is reason enough to join. So, unless you have appointments on your first day in this area, the Lake Chapala Society should be your first stop. Here's their website: lakechapalasociety.com. Their office is open from 10am to 2pm Monday through Saturday, but the grounds are open from 9 to 5.

"Renting, at least for the first six months or so, is probably still your best option, however."

Next, the real estate agents you've contacted will be happy to show you the various neighborhoods and houses. This will be a good time for you to interview your agents, too, since real estate agents in Mexico are not formally licensed or regulated. Anyone with the proper visa or citizenship can call him/herself a real estate agent. And, they are not obligated to tell you of any defects or other issues regarding properties. For instance, some old houses have pipes that are not wide enough to allow toilet paper to pass. Either you will have to be content with using a trash container for your used toilet paper, or you will be faced with a significant cost for upgrading the plumbing.

The only type of lawyers authorized to prepare real estate deeds and documents in Mexico are *Notario Públicos*, who will research and prepare your title and all the documents involved in the sale or financing transaction. See the Appendix for more information about Mexican lawyers. I can recommend Notaria 5. That's located in the orange stucco building at 245-D Hidalgo (that's the *carretera*—the main road) in Chapala. It's in the block just west of the main intersection of Hidalgo and Madero streets. They speak English there, and are easy to work with. The phone number is 376-765-2740.

Renting, at least for the first six months or so, is probably still your best option, however.

Reason #1: You won't be buying until you've had a chance to get the feel of different neighborhoods over time, and about the ways Mexican houses are different from the ones you're used to. Some neighborhoods are noisier than you may be used to, which is a common complaint of expats here. In some neighborhoods, people live fairly closely to each other, some have noisy guard-dogs, and some have bars and restaurants with live music at night. Some neighborhoods have an abundance of roosters who are confused about when dawn begins, and some have churches whose bells ring and whose loudspeakers start up at inconvenient hours. And, parking and traffic can be troublesome in some neighborhoods during the more crowded snowbird season. These are not show-stopping issues, however, since expats do live there, and most love it. Most just learn to live with them. But it's good to be aware of issues up front when you're choosing a place to live. Over time, the roosters, the church bells, the music, and the dogs simply blend into the tapestry of every-day life, just like the beautiful bird songs, the calls of the street vendors, the occasional mariachi band practices, the clopping of horses on the cobblestones, and the cicada chirps announcing the coming of the rainy season (June through October).

On the other hand, you may want to consider whether one of the gated communities here, inhabited primarily by other expats, would be right for you. These communities come with a few extra costs and rules for security and maintenance. You may not get the full flavor of Mexico you're looking for in these neighborhoods. You may feel too insulated, and the houses may look too much like the cookie-cutter suburban houses you didn't like north of the border. But, maybe you did like those houses, and maybe you would prefer a more familiar, secluded environment.

Your Exploratory Trip: During Your Trip

All of these are trade-offs that take time to consider before buying a house.

Reason #2: Renting frees up your time. Home ownership involves a lot of effort, responsibility, time, and money. If you're downsizing, consider letting go of home ownership. That's what I did. I loved my home and being a homeowner in the US, and I love my home and not owning it here.

Reason #3: Rental costs are comparatively low. A nice 2-bedroom rental house (*casita*) or apartment can still be found for around $600 (and even less in some neighborhoods). You'll need to pay for your first month's rent, last month's rent, and a month's security deposit up front. But nobody will look up or care about your credit history. That's freeing in itself. This is the land of new beginnings. All they need to see for identification is your passport.

Reason #4: Most rentals come fully furnished (or there might be an unfurnished option). When you relocate to this area, you will most likely not move all your belongings with you at first. It's comforting to know that you can take your time with the rest of your move, or that you can buy new furnishings as you find the ones you want, on your own schedule.

Reason #5: You will learn some invaluable information about Mexican houses before you actually invest in one. You will learn all about water tanks, water pressure, water purification systems, window types, ventilation, heating and cooling, propane gas tanks, insects, security, roofs, plumbing types, and how to work with Mexican construction workers.

If you decide to rent, it's best to work through a rental agency at first. They're fluent in English, and can help you in many ways as a newcomer. Plus, they're quite responsive regarding upkeep and repairs. They have repair people on staff or contract that are competent and trustworthy—and they even speak a little English. You'll want to check online for the most prominent rental agencies in this area, and telephone them. Be aware that in Mexico, landlords are not obligated to fix or upgrade anything unless there's a health or safety hazard. So, do make sure that your lease specifically states who is responsible for what, and what is included—especially if you rent from an independent landlord.

> *"Be aware that in Mexico, landlords are not obligated to fix or upgrade anything unless there's a health or safety hazard."*

Also, get a detailed list of the furnishings that are included with the house—a photographic representation is even better. Some agents "dress up" the house to rent it, but when you get there, the furniture is different, or perhaps there's a phone with no phone line.

And, do be candid about whether you'll be living with any pets. You'll find that landlords are much more accepting of pets here than they are north of the border, but there are some communities that do have pet (and children) restrictions, such as apartments and condos.

Of special interest on your lease is the subject of housekeepers and gardeners. Since most rental agencies also manage the properties, they often employ a housekeeper and/or a gardener who has worked at the house from one renter to another. Your lease should say whether your house has such arrangements, and whether those services are included in your monthly rental.

By the way, and this is **very important**, always use your name **exactly** as it looks on your passport for all your legal documents, including your lease, house purchase, tourist and visa documents, checking accounts, and vehicle documents. Don't use only your middle initial if your passport spells it out. This could save you a lot of trouble later.

Names can be complicated in Mexico. What looks like the middle name of a Mexican native is really the father's last name. And what looks like the last name is really the mother's last name. For example, Miguel Pedro Garcia Morales's mother's last name is Morales, and his father's last name is Garcia. His middle name is Pedro.

Most Mexicans actually call themselves by their middle name. This is because parents often use biblical saint names as the first name. It would not be uncommon for a family to have five boys whose first names are all Miguel. It's the middle name that differentiates each one. In the example above, he would probably call himself Pedro Garcia, using his middle name and his father's last name, except on legal documents.

> *"Always use your name exactly as it is spelled on your passport for all your legal documents."*

The important thing for you to remember is not to take middle names lightly— especially your own. Always make sure that no one uses your middle name mistakenly as your last name on documents.

Whether you decide to buy or rent, you'll find more housing available, and better prices, during the slow season (April through October) before the return of the snowbirds.

At this point, after having explored the area and available housing, and after having talked with all your contacts (agencies, B&B staff and guests, and the Lake Chapala Society), you should be able to decide whether your needs match what the Lake Chapala area has to offer. If your needs don't match, you have undoubtedly at least had an informative and interesting vacation stay. If your needs do match, *bienvenido* (welcome)!

Your Exploratory Trip: During Your Trip

Once I made this decision, I felt relieved and excited and panicked all at once, and then again in waves during the following weeks. The indecision was gone, and I was ready to move full speed ahead, but I didn't know quite what that entailed. My hope is that, with this book, you will be more prepared and informed than I was.

At this point, one of the key activities (aside from finding a place to live) you might want to undertake on your exploratory trip is to establish mailing addresses (to be used as forwarding addresses) for both letters and packages. Mexican postal system mail carriers only deliver flat mail (what they can reasonably carry on a motorcycle) directly to your address. If there's a package, the mail carrier will give you a claim slip for it to be picked up at the nearest post office. Many expats choose other options than delivery by the Mexican postal system, however, for many reasons. Please see the Index for additional information about mail. If, after reading about this topic, you decide you would like to use the services of a mail service company, now is a good time to make those arrangements so you can provide your current home post office with forwarding addresses before your actual move.

One other key activity you will want to undertake on your exploratory trip is to find a border driver, if you want one. When most people move here from north of the border, they pack their car full of their essentials, and drive across the border. I, for one, felt a little intimidated by the prospect of then driving through half of Mexico on my own, even though I had a GPS map of Mexico. It wasn't just the armed guards at the various checkpoints that I thought might be intimidating, but the fact that I didn't know very much Spanish or the traffic rules, or know which hotels allowed pets, or how to deal with potential car breakdowns or repairs.

> *"One other key activity you will want to undertake on your exploratory trip is to find a border driver."*

A border driver is an English-speaking Mexican national (usually) who will take a bus to the border, meet you there, and chauffeur your car (with you in it) to your new home. He (it's always a he) can help smooth the way at the checkpoints, the toll booths and gas stations, the restaurants (he'll know the best ones on the way), hotels and rest stops. And, he'll keep you company and give you lots of additional information, too, along the way. The cost varies, and is negotiable, although you should plan for around $500 USD. Your B&B staff may be able to recommend a driver to you. You can certainly make these arrangements

Your Exploratory Trip: During Your Trip

after your exploratory trip, but you might want to meet your driver first in order to feel comfortable with him.

One last important thing: be sure to take lots of photos and videos of your trip and of your new home. Your friends and neighbors will be much more comfortable with your move if they can see what you've seen—a beautiful, semi-tropical lake and mountain area, populated with lots of people like yourself, enjoying their lives among a warm and friendly local population.

Having said all this, I should also say that it's not strictly necessary for you to take an exploratory trip to Lake Chapala before your move. You can just drive down, find a B&B, and unload the contents of your vehicle in a storage unit here until you've found a place to live. Just Google "storage Chapala" to find a storage unit. You'll also want to ask your B&B staff about long-term off-street parking for your car within easy walking distance.

Part 2

Before Your Move

Now that you've made your decision to move to Lake Chapala, and you're back home wondering how you're going to pull it off, it might help you to know that there are really only a few main areas you need to think about at first: your finances, choosing a move date (which you may already have done), telling your family and friends, and deciding what to do about your pets and belongings. Everything else will fall into place naturally.

Chapter 1

Consider Your Finances

There are two aspects of your finances you'll need to consider: whether you will have enough money to make the move, and whether you will have enough money to stay.

If you're moving from either Canada or the US, and you're planning to drive with your initial belongings, the whole move will most likely cost between $6,000 and $10,000 USD. But don't panic! You will probably get that amount from the sale of your excess belongings. These figures include almost everything from your exploratory trip flight and expenses, pets (health checks), your drive down (car checkup, fuel, tolls, tourist card, vehicle border deposit and permit, motel, meals, border driver), your first and last month's rent and security deposit, establishing your new insurance, utilities and technology, and buying the basics of setting up your new house (food, cleaning items, waste baskets, light bulbs). It's after that initial outlay that you'll see the savings in your living expenses.

"If you're moving from either Canada or the US, and you're planning to drive with your initial belongings, the whole move will most likely cost between $6,000 and $10,000."

Before Your Move: Consider Your Finances

You can stay in Mexico forever on your tourist card, hypothetically, if you don't mind crossing the border every six months to have it and your vehicle permit re-issued for 180 more days. So far, border patrols have allowed this, but they could stop it at any time. There are increasing rumors that border patrols may start denying people who have done this a few times from repeating it. If they think you're obviously residing in Mexico and simply avoiding getting a resident visa (which is lucrative for Mexico), they could deny you re-entry until you have at least a visa application.

On a tourist card, no one will care where in Mexico you live, or how much money you have, and you can scrape by on very little. There are decent studio apartments, rooms, and shared housing here for as low at $275 per month. There are also people who need house-sitters for free rent while they're traveling. And if you're frugal in everything else, you could, conceivably, squeak by on $800 per person per month. That's on paper, of course. Only you know what creature comforts you have to have as a minimum, and how long you can comfortably keep that up.

But, as stated above, staying forever on renewed tourist status is no longer recommended since multiple renewals may not be possible in the future. And, living in Mexico illegally is not recommended either. Aside from the possibility of being deported, life would be much more difficult: no driver's license, no insurance, difficulty finding a decent place to rent, no bank account. Almost every transaction of this kind requires proof of being here legally.

As of 2017, the Mexican government requires a minimum income of 24,010 pesos (**$1,334 USD** at an exchange rate of 18.00) per person per month to qualify for a temporary residence visa (see Visas in the Index for additional information). Spouses and dependents need only show 25% of that amount.

What about working and earning money while you're here? Mexico's policies may limit a foreigner from taking a job that a Mexican could fill. But, if you do receive a job offer, you'll note that your pay will not be anywhere near what you would expect north of the border. Typically, it's about one-third. If you accept the job offer, the hiring company will help you get a special temporary residence visa (Residente Temporal) with working permission. That visa will become invalid, though, if you leave that company, unless you get hired by another one.

> *"As of 2017, the Mexican government requires a minimum income of 24,010 pesos ($1,334USD at an exchange rate of 18.00) per person per month to qualify for a temporary residence visa."*

Before Your Move: Consider Your Finances

If you move here and work for a non-Mexican company that has a physical presence in Mexico, you will also need a working visa, which that company will help you obtain. Again, your working permission will become invalid if and when you leave that company.

If you perform any other work than what is authorized by your visa—for example, serve on a board of directors or work for a non-profit organization without pay—you may need to have authorization from the immigration department. Be sure to check with the organization what the immigration status requirements are.

You could also work for yourself. In order to legally earn income, you need to be either a Mexican citizen, or have a Residente Permanente visa (see the Index for more information), or have a Residente Temporal visa with working permission, and be registered with the tax authority. If you want to hire employees, you should be aware that there's an informal policy of hiring on a 10 to 1 ratio of Mexicans to foreigners. You will need a lawyer's guidance regarding these issues, and for licenses and taxation.

Lastly, you could just work for under-the-table earnings. Lots of Mexicans and expats do. It could work out well for you, but if someone were to report you to the authorities, you could be fined and/or deported. Again, it's best to contact a lawyer to discuss your available options.

Chapter 2

Choosing Your Move Date

Choosing your move date first may seem a little rash. But it will serve several purposes.

1. Having a firm move date will focus your mind. The move will become a reality rather than a daydream—a reality whose tasks can't be procrastinated away.
2. Having a move date will strengthen your position and resolve as you discuss your move with friends and family, who may not be as excited as you are (at first).

If you're planning to rent a house or apartment at Lake Chapala, you'll need to sign a lease confirming a move-in date. If you're purchasing a house, you will be negotiating a date by which you can move in. So, you will probably have come home from your exploratory trip with at least an arrival date in mind. Using that date as a basis, work backward to arrive at a move date, depending on whether you're going to fly in or drive in.

Chapter 3

Telling Your Family and Friends

Most people I have talked to found this to be one of the most difficult aspects of the move. The first reason, of course, is that your family and friends will miss you. They're used to having you around. They would probably be upset if you moved to Paris, too. You will need to soothe their fears about your relationship with them, as well as explain how the move will benefit your life in other ways. You may want to share with them the list of needs you made in making your decision, and how you feel these needs will be met. And, you'll certainly want to share with them all the photos and videos you took on your exploratory trip.

The second reason that this could be difficult is that your friends and family may have heard bad publicity about crime in Mexico. What they may not fully realize is that Mexico is a big, diverse country, and that most areas of it are not only safe, but are fascinating places to visit and live.

There are over a million expats living in Mexico (most are from the US and Canada), and many of those live in expat communities like Lake Chapala. These communities have a blend of Mexicans and expats, and have the culture and feel of old Mexico, while growing technologically to accommodate modern needs. The major crime areas are along the northern border, and in parts of the southern Mexican states. There have been very few crimes reported involving tourists and expats—far fewer than would be experienced in, for instance, New Orleans or Chicago. The government is very happy to have expats come and spend money in Mexico without taking Mexican jobs, so they're very motivated to protect these communities. The police force responds quickly to issues that do occur—the occasional pick-pocket, or broken side mirror of a car, or a home burglary while someone is away. It's very rare that an expat gets hurt.

In this community, there are poor people living alongside well-to-do people. Sometimes the temptation to steal is overwhelming, especially if expensive-looking jewelry is worn or money is flashed imprudently. In general, I have found the Mexicans in this community to be friendly, conservative, helpful, hard-working, and very patient with all the small *faux-pas* we northerners inadvertently commit regarding their language, social etiquette, and customs. They also appreciate the economic benefits of our presence to their charities, infrastructure, and quality of life.

Your family and friends can do some additional internet research on the subject of expats living at Lake Chapala. The Appendix has a list of web boards, forums, and blogs. And, my online magazine Lake Chapala Reporter has a wealth of informative articles. You might also find a way to involve your friends and family in some way in your move, and to invite them to come and visit you in your new home.

Before Your Move: What About Your Pets?

Chapter 4

What About Your Pets?

I need hardly say that, to most people, pets are like family. It's difficult to imagine our lives without them once we have them. If you have been contemplating getting a new pet, wait until you get to your new home. You'll find many wonderful dogs, cats, horses, and birds of all ages in the Lake Chapala area ready to be adopted. There will undoubtedly be some stress in your household as you plan and conduct your move, and when you move in. The additional tasks and changes involved with having a new pet will only be more stressful for your household and the pet during this time.

"Dogs and cats are not quarantined when they come into Mexico if they are in good health."

The Lake Chapala area has a good selection of excellent veterinarians, very good pet foods (many US brands), and very good services (grooming and boarding). In upcoming sections, I'll describe the best ways to transport your pets, which paperwork is needed, and what you can expect at the border. But here are some considerations to help you make pet decisions at the outset.

1. Dogs and cats are not quarantined when they come into Mexico if they are in good health, and if they have the right paperwork (more on that later).
2. You're not allowed to bring in more than three pets per person, technically. Otherwise customs *may* decide that you're going to sell them in Mexico, in which case you will need to pay import duties on them. A reasonable number of pets isn't usually questioned, however, especially if you have other signs that you're actually moving to Mexico. To be safe, do not exceed the maximum of three pets per owner, as listed on the health certificates. Three more pets could be owned by another adult in the car, though.
3. Only you know whether taking your pet on a long trip is in its best interest, and yours. If your pet is very old or undergoing extensive medical treatments, you may want to delay your move rather than risk your pet's ability to withstand the move, or to be able to adjust to a new environment.
4. Reptiles (snakes, lizards) are not allowed to cross the border (except on their own, presumably). However, some turtles have been known to be let in (with health certificates).
5. Some birds can be brought in as pets, but they need special permission. Birds that are native to Mexico are prohibited, though. These include some parakeets, some macaws, and some parrots. For up-to-date lists and procedures, check

Before Your Move: What About Your Pets?

bit.ly/2weSW6A, or contact US Fish and Wildlife in Laredo, Texas. Phone number: 956-726-2234.

6. Be aware that bringing birds back into the US is not easy due to the many problems the US has had regarding smuggled birds—including the bird flu and Newcastle disease scares. US customs officials do not distinguish between parakeets and chickens. They're all birds. The paperwork is extensive, and there is an automatic 30-day quarantine for all live birds going into the US. If you don't want your birds to be quarantined, you will need to give away or sell your birds in Mexico if you decide to move back to the US later. There are also restrictions on bringing birds back into Canada. Here is more information: bit.ly/2lbROzj.

> *"There is an automatic 30-day quarantine for all live birds going into the US."*

7. Horses are not considered pets, and, as such, must be imported through a customs broker. Here is further information, see here: bit.ly/2xUOnkh and here: bit.ly/2f9n5i5.

The Mexican government has posted some information about bringing various dogs and cats into Mexico here: bit.ly/2eLNmSY.

Chapter 5

What About Your House?

If you currently rent your home, all you need to do is notify your landlord in writing when you plan to vacate your home. The amount of lead time you need to give your landlord will be noted in your lease.

If you own your home, you have four options, and they're more complicated.

Selling your house
This is the most logical option, of course. Since it may take a long time to sell, you may want to choose a real estate agent who is also willing to manage the property for you after you're gone. That way, prospective buyers won't be put off by seeing a tangle of long weeds instead a neat lawn. If you owe more on the house than it's worth on the market, you may qualify for what's known as a "short sale" (in the US, anyway), whereby the bank agrees to allow you to sell the house outright for less than you owe on it. Some banks are much more lenient in this regard than others. Be aware, though, that the "short sale" option does lower your US credit rating to some extent, if that's important to you. Your real estate agent can give you more information about this option. The benefits of selling your house are that you'll be able to get out from under it, and you may even end up having enough money to purchase a house in Mexico—a much nicer house for the money, in fact.

Renting your house

This could be a good option if you think you might return to your home country to live, and if the house would still be a good fit for you at that time. A big Victorian house with 3 stories wouldn't be good for an older person who might have difficulty with stairs, for instance. The amount you could rent the house for should be more than enough to cover your mortgage payment, taxes, all upkeep and maintenance, and the cost of an ongoing property manager. Don't take this option if your *only* reason is to wait to sell it until the housing market bounces back. If the house has been in the family for generations, for instance, you may want to consider having other family members live in it while you're gone, or get a trusted house-sitter. Or, it may be better to just get out from under the burden now, and to start fresh in your new environment.

Donating your house

If you own your house outright, and you're having trouble selling it, you can donate it to a non-profit organization in order to get a tax credit, instead. The non-profit organization can then fix up the house, and sell it later for its own charitable works. Here's an article about this option: bit.ly/2wNZ3Dt.

Walking away

This option is one that many homeowners take when they owe more on their mortgage than the house is worth on the market, and when they are willing to sacrifice their US credit rating for the next 7 to 10 years. Mexicans usually don't care about your US credit rating because most transactions are paid in cash. But walking away from your house could affect your ability to get financing for a Mexican house if the financing comes from your home country, or if you get a mortgage from a Mexican bank with an affiliate bank in the US. It would certainly also affect you if you were to return to your home country within those 7 to 10 years (whether you buy or rent, or wanted to buy a car, for instance.). This is a difficult decision. You may want to talk this over with your mortgage holder, a real estate agent in your home country, and a real estate agent in Mexico for all the implications.

> *"Mexicans don't care about your US credit rating because most transactions are paid in cash."*

Chapter 6

What About Your Car?

Should you take your car or buy one in Mexico? If you're coming from somewhere *other than* north of the border, it makes more sense to sell your car and buy one in Mexico. If you're coming from the US or Canada, this question has become more complicated with the 2012 immigration law changes. Holders of Residente Permanente visas may not import foreign-plated cars. That

> *"If you need your car to drive your belongings to Mexico, then it makes sense to bring it."*

part isn't new. But in the past, you could just delay getting a Residente Permanente visa until you were ready to get rid of your car and get a Mexican-plated one. But with the new immigration law, you can only have a Residente Temporal visa (the lead-up to the Residente Permanente visa) for four years (see Visas in the Index for more information).

If you need your car to drive your belongings to Mexico, then it makes sense to bring it, and worry about what to do with it later. If you're planning to remain a tourist (and not apply for a residence visa), you won't have any car complications later, as long as you renew your temporary car import permit every time you leave and re-enter Mexico (every 180 days). However, as stated earlier, this is not recommended since there may be restrictions in the future regarding how many times you can get a new tourist visa.

If you are thinking of applying for a Residente Temporal visa, you'll have four years to think about what to do with your car. If you're applying for a Residente Permanente visa, though, you're not allowed to import a foreign-plated car in Mexico. Some couples get around this restriction by one person remaining a Residente Temporal since spouses are allowed to drive each others' cars. If your car mechanic says your current car is on its last legs, though, get a different one that will withstand the trip, but don't get a brand new one. That's because you're not officially allowed to sell a foreign-plated vehicle in Mexico.

> *"Holders of Residente Permanente visas may not import foreign-plated cars."*

There is a loophole around this, though, where you can sell a foreign-plated car to another foreigner in Mexico (Mexicans are not allowed to own or drive foreign-plated cars). The way it's done is to have the title changed to the buyer's name, as you normally would do north of the border, and then have the buyer order a temporary car import permit online. Mexican authorities will never know that the sale actually occurred in Mexico because they will not have a record of the original owner.

Before Your Move: What About Your Car?

You can also officially import your vehicle at the border. It's expensive (a couple of thousand US dollars), there's lots of fraud, some vehicles don't qualify, and car insurance for Mexican cars is more expensive. So, unless you're inordinately attached to your car, or it's brand new, plan on either selling your foreign-plated car to another foreigner in Mexico using the loophole mentioned above, or drive it into the ground in Mexico (but only for four years) because the only things you'll be able to do with it after that are:

"You can't legally sell a foreign-plated vehicle in Mexico."

1. surrender it to Hacienda (the Mexican treasury), if they'll take it
2. sell it to a junk yard for next to nothing
3. drive it back to the US and sell it
4. officially import it, if it qualifies. See the Index under Vehicles - Nationalizing regarding vehicle importation qualifications and fees.

Actually, there is one other option that some people use in order to keep their imported cars. That is to get license plates from another Mexican state, like Michoacan or the state of Mexico. It costs between 6,000 and 8,000 pesos, and it's not really legal. That is, the federal system still has a record of the car as being foreign. Local *transitos* (traffic police) do not have access to that system, however. So, for routine traffic stops, there would be no problem. If the car

49

were to be involved in an accident, though, or be stopped by federal or immigration police, the car would probably be confiscated, unless some compensation (bribery) could be arranged. Local car mechanics are probably the best sources of information regarding how to get these out-of-state license plates.

Only one car, SUV, RV motor home, or pickup truck (including a motorcycle carried on the bed, or on an attached trailer) **per person** is allowed a vehicle permit when crossing into Mexico. The only exception is that a vehicle being towed by an RV motor home may be owned by the same person that owns the RV motor home (which, incidentally, can usually get a 10 year permit.). If you're a couple, though, and you want to bring in two vehicles, make arrangements for the other vehicle to be driven across the border by the other person.

A new car used to costs more in Mexico than in the US or Canada because of import duties, but that is no longer the case because of improved currency exchange rates, even considering Mexico's 16% national sales tax. Car prices are now about the same.

If you're going to use a moving company, and you want to avoid the hassle of disposing of your car in four years (probably having to drive it north of the border to sell it), it makes more sense to sell your car before you move, and to buy a Mexican-plated one once you've arrived. Most people from north of the border still drive across the border

Before Your Move: What About Your Car?

in their current car, however, because most of them use it to move their belongings.

Chapter 7
What About Your Other Belongings?

This subject might seem overwhelming at first, but it all falls into place as time goes on. And, you'll even become more accepting of letting things go, too. This is a great time to simplify your life and to downsize. Possessions will seem much less important to you in Mexico (believe it or not), and friends, experiences, beauty, and nature will become much more important. For now, just categorize your major possessions. If you're computer savvy, build a spreadsheet. Here are some high-level categories.

1. To give to family and friends
2. To take to Mexico
3. To ship to Mexico
4. To sell
5. To donate to charity
6. Not sure yet

Give to family and friends
If you're planning to leave items to anyone in your will, consider doing that now, instead. You're probably not going to need (or even want) your extensive jewelry collection, your 32 place-settings of sterling flatware, or grandma's trunk of lace doilies. In fact, you probably won't need anything that's in your attic, including your winter clothes.

Take to Mexico

After you've come close to determining which things to give to your family and friends, you'll know which items are left. Here's where you need to make a big decision: whether to take only what you can ship or fit into your pick-up truck, RV, car or SUV, and get rid of everything else, or to (eventually) bring all your remaining possessions to Mexico.

Using an international moving company to move a 3 bedroom household of furniture by truck from midwest US to Lake Chapala will cost about $20,000. Only you know whether that's worthwhile for you. You can buy an awful lot of furniture in Mexico for that amount of money. And, keep in mind that your King Louis XIV chairs may look out of place in a more rustic setting. If you'd like an estimate of your moving costs, there are companies that are very good and experienced at this. One such company is Strom–White Moving Company (www.strommoving.com). Another one is Lake Chapala Moving Company (www.lakechapalamoving.com. You can find others on the internet, as well. And, if you live along a coast, you may

"Using an international moving company to move a 3 bedroom household of furniture by truck from midwest US to Lake Chapala will cost about $20,000."

save money by asking your moving company about shipping your possessions by boat.

Be aware, though, that moving companies sometimes give very low estimates in order to get the winning bid, but then they come up with creative fees at the end of the trip. It's best to eliminate very low bids for that reasons, or to put a maximum amount (say, 10%) of overage fees right into your contract. That's an especially good idea for moving companies who charge by weight rather than volume. After all your furniture is loaded onto their trucks, they take a final weight, and (surprise!) the weight is much higher than the estimate they gave you. At that point, everything you own is on their truck, and you're on a schedule to leave. So you might be trapped at that point. You'll also want to ask about tips for the crew. Sometimes they're mandatory. Do read the fine print in the moving contract.

Another option is to have your things moved into a storage space near the US – Mexican border. Then, whenever you or your friends and family cross the border in the future, more things can be brought down, usually without paying import duties. It's a lot more effort and time, of course, but it may be worth it to you.

Most people I've talked to decided to take only what they could fit into their pickup truck, RV motor home, SUV, or car—and to ship some bulky items, like books. You'll be surprised how much your car or SUV can hold. You could even add a (locking) roof carrier to the top. Identify now

Before Your Move: What About Your Other Belongings?

which items have strong meaning for you that you can't imagine living without. In this category might be family letters and photos (you could have these digitized in advance), memorable trinkets, your favorite guitar, and favorite books (more about books later)—and, of course, your pets and your valuable documents. You might want to get an expandable plastic file folder now, and start collecting your valuable documents in it. Don't forget the contents of your safety deposit box.

> *"The electrical plugs are exactly the same as in the US and Canada, including the 3-pronged grounded ones."*

In addition to taking your favorite items, you'll also want to take items that are hard to find Mexico. Among these are electronics. They're available here, but keyboards, for instance, are Mexican. The electrical plugs are exactly the same as in the US and Canada, including the 3-pronged grounded ones.

DVRs aren't really used here, and are extremely hard to find since there's no standard schedule coding of programs. You could certainly use the one you have for taping on a timed basis, though.

> *"DVRs aren't really used here, since there's no schedule coding of programs."*

55

And, be aware that DVDs and DVD players are coded for specific regions of the world. For instance, Canada and the US are Region 1, and Mexico is Region 4. You might want to check your DVD player and DVR documentation to see which regions they support. All the pirated DVDs here do seem to be able to be played on US DVD players, though.

If you're a computer user, you'll want to bring a laptop (with an American keyboard). High-quality all-in-one printer/copier/fax/scanners are plentiful here, so those are optional. You could bring your wireless land phones. If you sew, you could bring your sewing machine. If you have a good tool collection, bring that, too. But, these are all available here, too.

> *"To prevent customs agents at the border from charging you duty fees on new electronics, take new items out of their boxes, and smear a little peanut butter or dirt on the cords to make them look used."*

By the way, in order to prevent customs agents at the border from charging you duty fees on new electronics, take new items out of their boxes, and smear a little peanut butter or dirt on the cords to make them look used.

You could also bring your favorite set of dishes, cookware set, and flatware, plus your favorite kitchen gadgets. Be aware that Mexico's units of measure are in metrics. For example,

Before Your Move: What About Your Other Belongings?

pitchers here have markings for liters, not quarts. You won't need to bring your microwave, coffee maker, toaster oven, or any other small kitchen appliances, except maybe your favorite Cuisinart food processor. Most small kitchen appliances, as well as personal electrical appliances (hair dryers, etc.) are readily available here, and are not very expensive.

Most Mexican houses do not have a lot of carpets and rugs, so you probably won't need your vacuum cleaner. What they do have is tiles—miles and miles of tiles, which are nice and cool in this semi-tropical climate.

Of course, you'll want to decide which jewelry to bring. You'll really only use the simplest of jewelry. No one wears large cocktail rings, rhinestones, and flashy bling here. Do bring your favorite conservative, classy pieces (especially natural materials, like turquoise), and consider giving away or selling the rest. Costume jewelry is best.

Regarding clothing, you'll want to take mostly summer clothing, including a couple of sweaters and jackets for cool evenings. You can safely give away or donate everything else.

If you think that all of these items won't fit in your SUV, they all fit into my Jeep along with two big book-boxes of photos, two cats, a cat carrier, two medium dogs, two dog beds, and three 12-packs of Diet Dr. Pepper—all without a rooftop carrier. It can be done!

Ship to Mexico

Consider shipping items to Mexico that are too big or too numerous to fit in your vehicle.

There is a US mail category specifically for shipping books internationally. It's called USPS Airmail M-Bags. It's not cheap, but it is cheaper than regular international shipping methods. You pack your books in your own boxes so that they're less than 66 lbs each. Each box must be labeled as if you were going to ship it by itself. Then, take the boxes to a post office approximately 3 weeks before your move (they'll take from 4 to 6 weeks to arrive), and they'll be put in canvas bags and tagged. The cost to Mexico is $46.20 for a bag weighing 11 pounds or less, plus $4.20 per additional pound up to 66 pounds. So, it's about $277 for a 66 pound bag—about $4.20 per pound. Here is more information about shipping your books via Airmail M-Bags: bit.ly/1jgrb7K. If you're not in the US, check with your post office about any special international book mailing services from your home country.

Another category of items is paintings. You'll want to pack them carefully in your car, if you can, but you may also want to ship some of them. If you decide to do that, the paintings must be quite valuable to you. In that case, have a professional crate them for you for shipping, with light metal panels on the sides for protection. Don't count on the crates being babied along the route. No matter how much you label them "Fragile—handle with care," they're going to be treated nonchalantly. Compare the shipping rates between major freight carriers who deliver here, like Federal Express, UPS, and DHL—and have the paintings insured.

There are many excellent artists in this area, doing fascinating work, so do consider that you'll want to add Mexican art to your home. Reduce the number of art pieces and paintings you bring to the bare minimum.

Sell

This will probably be your largest category of items. You might be tempted to just have a big yard sale, but that will not be the best option for most of your items unless you're in a hurry and just want to get rid of everything, taking anything left over to a charity.

If you have any unique or valuable pieces, consider auctioning them on eBay, if you know how to do that. Be sure to set an appropriate minimum dollar amount so you don't regret selling it if you only get the minimum bid. And do start the process early enough so that you will have time to try auctioning it several times.

"You might be tempted to just have a big yard sale, but that will not be the best option for most of your items unless you're in a hurry and just want to get rid of everything, taking anything left over to a charity."

If eBay is not a good option for you, your next-best option is to have your items auctioned by professional auctioneers. Phone one or two of the most reputable auction houses in your area (just Google "auction" and the name of your city), and have them come to your house to see what you have to sell. Make sure that they deal in general household furniture rather than just antiques. Also make sure they're registered, insured, and bonded. And, make sure that they take bids from prospective bidders by phone. That opens up the bidding to long distance and international buyers. What auctioneers will do is sell your items for you for about 30% of the total selling price (they get 30%, you get 70%). They'll do that by either moving your items to their auction house and conducting an auction there along with other peoples' items, or by having what's known as an estate auction.

An estate auction is conducted at your house, and is done if you have a large number of items to sell, and if you have decorated your house in such a way as to display the items to their best advantage. There are positives and negatives to each type of auction. In both cases, the auctioneers will take photos of your items, and post them on their websites. The photos are then looked at by prospective buyers—around the world, in many cases. This is why you'll get better prices than at a yard sale, where your buyers are usually just the people in your neighborhood.

Before Your Move: What About Your Other Belongings?

For an estate sale, you'll probably save a little money by not having to pay for the auctioneers to move your items to their facility. But, you will have lots of company for awhile. The auctioneers will come first to price and tag everything, and then, usually over the course of a weekend, you'll get a parade of people coming through your house, which doesn't appeal to everyone. You can either be there or not. If you're there, be prepared to hear positive and negative comments about your house, your yard, your taste, and the quality and value of your items. Whether you're there or not, you'll need to make other arrangements for your children and pets on those days.

> *"There's less chance of theft in the auctioneer's facility because of the security cameras and the locked display cases."*

Some thefts do occur at estate auctions because the items will be located throughout your house without the security cameras that auction houses have at their own facilities. Extra staff for monitoring each room may be offered, or not. But the staff is not well paid, so that in itself could be a problem. Or, you could have your own friends and relatives monitor the various rooms, too. You will then have buyers carrying their new treasures out of your house into their waiting pickup trucks, scratching your walls and stepping on your rose bushes (you may not care at this point, though).

Another negative to having an estate auction in your home is that strangers will see what else you have in your home, so you may feel a little vulnerable after that. Despite these negatives, lots of people choose this option because the items are not competing with other peoples' items for attention, and may get higher prices by being shown in a warm home environment. You can choose what to do with the items that are left over after the weekend's sale.

If you have the auction in the auctioneer's facility, many of the estate auction's negative considerations disappear. You will have your near-empty house to yourself after paying the auctioneers to move the items to their facilities. This arrangement is really called consignment. You'll be paying them a fee to sell your items. Again, you can choose whether to be present at the auction or not. There's less chance of theft in the auctioneer's facility because of the security cameras and the locked display cases. More people may show up because there will be other peoples' items up for bidding, too. However, your items will be competing for their attention and their spending dollars.

Regarding theft in either scenario, the auctioneers should be insured, so you will be reimbursed, but maybe not at the auction price you were hoping for. Whatever doesn't sell on the auction day is usually grouped together in lots and sold on another day with lower starting bids until everything is gone. This is good in that everything gets sold, but bad in that you don't have control of these remainders anymore. You may have been able to sell the

Before Your Move: What About Your Other Belongings?

remainders yourself at a yard sale for more. But again, you may not care so much at this point.

In either scenario, you'll get a check for 70% of the total winning bids in about a week after the auction. If you're going to be gone by then, make sure you give the auction house your new address, or the address of someone you trust who can deposit the check into your bank account, avoiding the lengthy travel time and hold a Mexican bank places on an out-of-country check (between 10 and 15 business days), and the fees many Mexican banks charge for a check deposit.

Auction houses usually do not take clothes, except for furs, in some cases. There's just not a great market for used clothes (at least not in the US), so these will sell best at a local consignment shop, or at a yard sale. Or donate them to a non-profit organization for a tax deduction. Do not ship them to Mexico, whether for yourself or to donate to a Mexican charity. It's illegal to ship or mail used clothing into Mexico.

"It's illegal to ship or mail used clothing into Mexico."

Your last option to sell is, of course, having a yard sale. Not much needs to be said about this, since you've probably done it before, and there are lots of good articles on the internet about how to have a successful one.

Donate to charity

You've probably donated clothes and small articles to Goodwill and the Salvation Army (in the US) all along. But do also consider donating to local shelters and food banks. They can sometimes use old shelves, paint, tools, bags, garden equipment, decorative items (posters, prints), kitchenware, and many other items you may not have thought of. Call a few of them and ask if they have lists of needed items. You'll feel great about having made these donations whether or not you receive a tax deduction.

Chapter 8

Four Weeks Before Moving

Up until this time, you've been planning and making decisions. But now you'll need to be on a countdown because some activities need to get started now. In fact, I would say that you could accomplish your entire move in one month from when you made the decision to move to the actual moving day if you're in a hurry. If you're at all inclined to make lists, now is the time to develop a spreadsheet in order to stay organized and on schedule. You'll be much less stressed, and you'll be confident that you haven't forgotten anything.

If you're interested in getting a Mexican residence visa, as opposed to just crossing the border as a tourist for up to 180 days, you have to apply at a Mexican consulate in your home country first. Sometimes they require an advance appointment. For people north of the border, the consulate does not have to be in your home state. It's best to apply as soon as possible because you may want to go to a second consulate if the first one you go to does not qualify you for a visa. Consulates sometimes interpret the requirements differently. The Las Vegas one and the Laredo, Texas one, for instance, are very lenient. Check the Index for specific visa requirements.

If the Mexican consulate in your home country approves your application for a residence visa, you will get a special

Canje (exchange) visa sticker on your passport. Then you will have 6 months to enter Mexico, and 30 days after that to exchange the Canje document you will get at the border for a real visa card once you're in Mexico.

If you plan to enter Mexico as a tourist, and you plan to drive here, make sure your driver's license has at least 6 months left on it, unless you're sure you can renew it by mail. The best idea is just to renew it, anyway, in order to get the maximum time. You can only get a Mexican driver's license if you have a residence visa, and Mexico requires a current driver's license—from any country.

If you're planning to take your car, you will need a temporary vehicle import permit (TIP). You can get one at the border, or you can get one in advance online. The cost is the same ($52 USD), but it will minimize your hassle at the border if you already have it. It takes about 4 business days to receive it in the mail. The website is: bit.ly/1pEB1vx.

If you rent your home, you should provide written notice to your landlord now (if you need to give 30 days' notice). You'll also want to make arrangements for any house inspection, and for the return of your security deposit. If you own your home, you will have made a decision about your house by this time. It should be listed for sale or rent now, or arrangements should be finalized to donate it.

Now is also the time to ship items or to give to your family and friends the items you have decided to give them. Then,

Before Your Move: Four Weeks Before Moving

contact one or two good consignment shops (you can find them online) to determine which clothes might be worth trying to sell. Start selling them now. Also, give your home a preliminary clean-out. Get rid of junk and piles of old newspapers.

If your finances are complicated, it's a good idea to have a talk now with your accountant about how to tie up loose ends and/or manage your assets when you're in Mexico. You will also want to make sure that your will is up to date.

For basic banking, many people just use their existing home bank debit or credit cards to withdraw pesos from ATMs in Mexico. ATMs automatically provide the best currency exchange rate. If that's what you'd like to do, keep in mind that you'll need to make a bank wire transfer to Mexico for any amounts larger than your daily maximum credit card withdrawal amount (which you might want to try to get increased now). There's a bank fee (around $15 USD) for a wire transfer. This is the simplest arrangement, provided your credit card is a common type, such as Visa, Visa Plus, MasterCard, Cirrus, or Pulse.

"You'll also want to inquire whether your bank has an arrangement with any Mexican banks to use their ATMs here without a transaction fee."

You'll also want to inquire whether your bank has an arrangement with any Mexican banks to use their ATMs here without a transaction fee (ATM transaction fees vary widely, depending on the bank). For instance, Bank of America has an arrangement that allows free ATM transactions at Santander and Scotiabank ATMs here. Also, try to get two copies of your ATM card in case one gets lost. In any case, don't close your home country checking account or give up your existing debit or credit card yet. It may take awhile to open a Mexican bank account because of new anti-money-laundering regulations. And, you'll find that Mexican banks are not as efficient as they are north of the border.

> *"Don't close your home country checking account or give up your existing debit or credit cards yet."*

Some Mexican banks require you to have a residence visa in order to open a new account. One that does not is Bancomer bank, which only requires a valid passport.

As soon as you get to Mexico, you'll want to at least know how to count and to understand spoken numbers in Spanish. It comes up surprisingly quickly, and you'll be thankful if you take some time to learn the numbers in advance. Many prices are negotiable in Mexico, and you won't want to overpay just because you don't understand what a vendor is saying. Most vendors are honest, but a few

Before Your Move: Four Weeks Before Moving

might be inclined to increase prices if they suspect you won't know the difference between a quote of 800 pesos and 80 pesos. So start learning your Spanish numbers now in your spare time. Buy some index cards and make flash cards (English on one side, Spanish on the other) of the numbers found on this video: bit.ly/2xYpfZK. Practice them until you know them by sight and sound, and can say them, too. Translate in both directions. Don't worry too much about precise pronunciation at this point. They sound pretty much like they look, except that Vs are pronounced like Bs. So, *veinte* (twenty) is pronounced "bayn'teh." Learn the hundreds, too, up to a thousand (*mil*). This is one of those activities that you might think is not very important right now. But, please trust me on this, you'll regret not doing it. I did.

Now is also the time to think about health insurance. There is much to be said on this subject later, but for now, it's important to know two things: 1) that US Medicare does not extend to Mexico, and 2) that if you buy private health insurance in Mexico, there will be a 60-day waiting period.

What's important now is that you don't cancel your existing health insurance, but make sure that it stays active at least 60 days after your move date (preferably 90 days, if you can afford it). You'll want to check with your health insurance provider as to how they handle emergency benefits while you're on "vacation" in Mexico. If anything catastrophic were to happen to you within the 60 day waiting period for your new insurance, you would probably need to pay medical expenses at the time of treatment, and then submit a reimbursement claim, saying you were on a Mexican vacation (whether or not you choose to go back to the US for further treatment).

Mexican law requires you to have car insurance. It would be utter folly not to have it since it's relatively inexpensive, and it could prevent you from being held in police custody until all liability is paid in full in the event of an accident (see the Index for Vehicles Insurance). Check now with your car insurance company to find out if driving in Mexico is covered by your policy (it probably isn't). Just as important is whether there is an agent available (24/7) to come to the scene of an accident in Mexico, which there probably won't be. But this is how things are done here. The car insurance agent (or a sub-contracted agent) must show up at the scene of an accident to represent you and to take financial responsibility, even if you have proof of insurance.

> *"One of the most important things you will need to do if you are married is to have your marriage license certified."*

One of the most important things you will need to do if you are married is to have an acceptable validation of your marriage license. My lawyer told me a sad story of a Canadian expat couple in Mexico. The husband had a heart attack and died. The wife could not prove she was the lawful spouse because her marriage certificate had not been certified, so she could not claim responsibility for the body. She had to get her marriage license certified in Canada by mail and courier, which took 2 weeks at a cost of $900 in fees and services. The moral of the story is to do it now before you leave. If you are in the US, a certified document is called an apostille, and it is obtained through your state's Secretary of State office. Just Google "apostille" and your state name, and you will find instructions online. You can get an apostille of many different types of documents that may pertain to you (adoption papers, birth certificates). In Canada, it's called "legalizing" a document. It is very difficult to do it from outside of Canada, so it's important to do this in advance. See this website for more information: bit.ly/2vOneOg.

Start now to collect all your important papers in one location, preferably in a portable, expandable, plastic file folder that you'll carry with you across the border. Include at this point (there'll be more later):

- Passport
- Temporary vehicle import permit (TIP), if you've applied for it online and received it
- Social Security card
- Social Security retirement benefit statement
- Investment documents
- Mexican house lease or purchase papers
- Next of kin and emergency numbers

Also include these documents, which need to be apostilled or legalized.

- Birth certificate
- Certified marriage license/civil union document
- Divorce papers
- Adoption papers

Chapter 9

Three Weeks Before Moving

If and when you decide to get private health insurance in Mexico, they will want to see two years' history of any significant medical conditions (heart disease, cancer, diabetes, hypertension, depression). That doesn't mean they'll exclude those conditions or increase your policy rates, necessarily, but they do want to know about them in advance. So, contact each doctor you've seen in the last two years, and tell him/her that you need their written notes, x-ray reports, and lab results for the last two years. If any of the x-rays showed anything significant, see if you can get the actual x-ray in addition to the radiologist's report.

From your dentist, all you need to ask for is your most recent set of x-rays, and any recent notes regarding work done. Dental records don't need to go back two years because they're not required by the health insurance companies. File all these documents in your portable file folder.

Another task to start now is to make sure all your bills are being paid automatically or online. The goal is that by the time you notify your post office of your new address in Mexico, there will be little or nothing to actually forward. Review your checking account and your stack of invoices and bills to see which merchants you're still paying by mail. Some of them can be paid right on the merchant's website, instead. For the rest, you'll want to set up online bill paying on your banks' online banking site. It's easy and reliable, and usually free. You may have written your last check— they're not used very much in Mexico.

If you have magazine subscriptions, you'll want to check whether they're available in digital format instead (on your PC or other devices). The hardcopy versions will not be automatically forwarded internationally.

You'll also want to make note of your favorite mail-order catalogs so you can visit those merchants online later instead of waiting for their catalogs in the mail. The catalogs won't be automatically forwarded internationally.

If you live near an IKEA store, buy some of their giant blue plastic shopping bags. You'll love them for open-air flea markets (*tianguis*) here, where there are no shopping carts. Those fruits and vegetables, flowers, bakery, fish, and what-nots get heavy. You can sling one bag over each shoulder. And get some for your partner, too. You'll be glad you did. They're great for moving, too.

> *"If you live near an IKEA store, buy some of their giant blue plastic shopping bags."*

You will also want to decide now which books you want to take with you in your car, and which ones you want to ship. For books to be shipped, keep in mind that you'll pay

Before Your Move: Three Weeks Before Moving

approximately $4.20 per pound. Set the ones for shipping aside now, and get some boxes for them. The book boxes from moving companies like U-Haul are best because they're the right size for books, and they're heavy duty. Pack the boxes tightly (no wiggle room), and tape them with reinforced strapping tape—not just clear shipping tape. They're going to go through a rough ride.

Label each box as if you're going to ship it separately, with the destination address and a return address. You'll want to use someone else's return address in your home country, just in case. There's no point having them returned to the address you're leaving. You can take them to the post office for M-Class shipping either this week or next. They'll take from 4 to 6 weeks to get to you in Mexico. You'll get a notice from your post office in Mexico when they're ready to be picked up.

Also, do contact your current cell phone carrier now to find out what to expect when you use your phone in Mexico. If it uses a 3G or 4G network, it will work in Mexico—for an added fee. It's called roaming. Find out how to turn roaming on and off on your devices for both voice and data (cell phones pass location data back and forth in the background automatically on the network), and how much extra it will cost.

If you have a smartphone or an electronic tablet, you'll also want to install the **Google Translate** application on it. It's free. It translates words between any two of 90 languages.

> *"If you know you'll be arriving at your new home in Mexico in the evening, and you don't have your new house keys yet, you will want to make arrangements with your new landlord or real estate agent to give your border driver the keys to bring with him."*

You can either type the word or speak it, and it will pronounce the word for you, too. It's very handy. But this requires an internet connection—either 3G or 4G if you're out in the open, or a wireless LAN if you're in a wi-fi hotspot. It also has a feature whereby you can hold your device's camera lens up to a sign or document, and it will translate the words on it in real time. It's quite amazing to see. This feature does not require an internet connection, so you can use it anywhere. I've used it for menus, signs at the park, contracts, and my Mexican cell phone instruction manual.

You will also want to install a GPS app like Google Maps or Waze so you can find the border and Lake Chapala from where you are, in case you're going to drive. It's also very handy for finding your way around Lake Chapala and on day trips.

You'll also want to contact your border driver this week to confirm your meeting point date and location. And, get his cell phone number in addition to his email address. This

Before Your Move: Three Weeks Before Moving

will come in handy as you're trying to locate each other at the border.

And, if you know you'll be arriving at your new home in Mexico after business hours, and you don't have your new house keys yet, make arrangements with your new landlord or real estate agent to give your driver the keys to bring with him.

"If your DVD player gets lost or broken in the process of moving, you won't be able to play your unfinalized DVDs on a new player."

By the way, be aware that Mexican cell phone numbers have a different format than you would expect. See the Index for Telephone Dialing.

And finally, you'll want to make sure that the homemade DVDs you're taking with you are "finalized" (check your user manual about how to do this). If your DVD player gets lost or broken in the process of moving, you won't be able to play your unfinalized DVDs on a new player.

Chapter 10

Two Weeks Before Moving

During this week, you will want to get a two-month supply of your normal medications. The only reason for getting that much is that you're going to be so busy with other details during the first month of moving in, you'll be glad you don't have to think about your medications, or about going to a new doctor for awhile. Most doctors and health plans will allow their patients to get a two-month supply of drugs for when they go on extended vacations.

Another task for this week is to purchase any pet carriers you may need. If you're going to fly your pets into Mexico, check with the airlines for specifications. The hard-cased carriers are almost all labeled as to whether they meet airline specifications. Just make sure your pet can stand, sit, and lay down comfortably in the size you choose. If you're going to drive dogs across the border, you probably don't need carriers. You just need a comfortable place for them to lie down. What I did was place their soft beds on top of large plastic bags of folded clothes in the back of my SUV. The bags made a nice flat surface for the beds, and added some cushioning for them, too.

Transporting cats is a little trickier unless they're housetrained and will go to the bathroom on a leash (highly unlikely). You probably won't want them loose in your car for fear of not only having soiling accidents, but that they'll

Before Your Move: Two Weeks Before Moving

get loose and run away when you open a door. So, you'll need a cat carrier that can contain a litter box plus food and water. What I found was a soft sided one with nylon and mesh on the sides and a full zipper at the front. I put a 13" by 9" sheet cake pan with kitty litter in it in the back of the carrier, and the food and water along the sides. I fit two cats in there very well. You'll also want a smaller, foldable carrier just for transporting the cats up and down from your motel room because the "car" carrier won't be strong enough to manage carrying the cats running around and the heavy sand. This arrangement, while it was time consuming to maintain, worked very well for me on the road.

During this week, you'll also want to make appointments for next week with your veterinarian for all your animals. They'll need to be brought up to date on their vaccinations, and the vet will need to certify on an international health form (make sure she has forms there) that the animals are up to date on their shots, that they're healthy, and that they don't have any parasites. If you're flying the animals across the border, the international health forms should be dated no more than 3 days before the flight (you may be able to persuade your veterinarian to leave the date blank for you to fill in later). If you're driving, try for no more than 10 days before you'll be crossing the border. Some sources say you have up to 30 days in advance when you're driving, but why take a chance?

Regarding your home: you'll want to leave it clean for the next person moving in. So, if you can afford it, hire a cleaning person now to do that for you sometime in the last few days before your move. You'll be surprised how much there will be to clean after all your furniture is removed.

Now is also a good time to notify your post office about stopping your mail. If you live in the US, you can do it online here: bit.ly/1Wmd4uU.

You can either provide your new Mexican address to the post office or not. If you choose not to, all mail (except junk mail, which will be discarded) will be returned to the sender. By this time, you should have notified everyone you want to what your new address is.

You can also tell your newspaper subscription folks now when to stop your deliveries. That can be done by phone.

And now for copies. In Mexico, it seems you need copies for almost everything. Even though almost all significant businesses have computers, they still like to have copies of transactions with your signature on them, and then they use rubbers stamps on them. Unfortunately, it's usually only stationery stores (*papelarías*) that make copies—for a peso or two. If you go to a bank, for instance, and they tell you that you need two copies of something, you might wonder why they don't just go in the back and make a few copies. It just doesn't work that way. It costs money. You will probably be directed to the nearest *papelaria* (if you ask), and then you'll have to come back again.

Before Your Move: Two Weeks Before Moving

It will be easier to make some copies now (before you move) of some documents that require internet access (which might take a little while to re-establish after you move).

For your border crossing into Mexico, you'll need some copies for your file folder. You'll want 3 copies of:

- your passport (the face and signature pages)
- your pets' international health documents

Plus, if you're driving, also make 3 copies of:

- your temporary vehicle importation permit, if you ordered it online
- your driver's license
- your car registration
- your car title

Chapter 11

One Week Before Moving

This is the last week of getting rid of all the things that you won't be taking with you. You might want to start a pile in one area of the house with everything you're going to take in the car. You can start packing clothes now, but you won't want to unplug your computer, TV, or phones until the last day, of course.

You'll want to clean out the clutter from your car this week, if you're driving, and take it for a mechanical inspection at your local repair shop. Make sure all the fluids are topped off, including windshield wiper fluid. Also, make sure they fill the tires with air at the correct pressure, that the tires are in good shape, and that you have a good spare tire.

> *"Print out a copy of the Jalisco and Mexico federal traffic laws located in the Appendix."*

Also, you might want to print out a copy of the Jalisco and Mexico federal traffic laws located in the Appendix (or just keep this book in your car)

At home, use up the groceries in your refrigerator, pantry and cabinets. If you have time, donate what you won't be using to a local shelter or food bank.

Before Your Move: One Week Before Moving

Be aware that any medications that don't have a prescription label are considered contraband, no matter how innocuous the medication is. It's a very serious crime to bring drugs like pain medications and amphetamines into Mexico which have not been issued by prescription.

Also, you must get rid of all weapons and ammunition before you cross the border. Make sure you don't have a single bullet anywhere—not even in the pocket of your favorite hunting jacket. You will have a small army of assault rifles escorting you to the nearest Mexican jail if you do. And you will be staying there for a long time.

Call your bank and credit card companies, and advise them that you're going to be traveling so they won't decline transactions when they see unusual locations or activities on your account. Make sure the notation will be effective for all your accounts.

"Call your bank and credit card companies, and advise them that you're going to be traveling so they won't decline transactions when they see unusual locations or activities on your accounts."

Withdraw enough cash from your bank now to get you to the border. If you can, pay any hotel bills, gas, and tolls in cash in order to avoid having to deal with any suspicious charges later.

Take your pets to the vet, and have an international health certificate filled out for each of them. If possible, have the vet leave the date blank so you can date it just before crossing the border. Also, ask to have a copy of your pets' medical records to take with you.

You might want to get a haircut and get your nails done now, so you won't have to think about them again for awhile. However, haircuts and manicures and artificial nails are less expensive at Lake Chapala.

Then pack, pack, and pack.

On your last day before moving, make arrangements for a house walkthrough, the return of house keys, and the return of any security deposit. Plus, if you're driving:

- contact your border driver, if you have one, to confirm your meeting day and time at the border,
- go to the store and buy sandwiches, fruit, snacks, and beverages for your trip, and
- load your car as much as possible before tomorrow.

Part 3

Your Move

"Part 3" is a fitting title here because, if you're like many expats living in Mexico's Lake Chapala area, you're in the third part of your life. This is a time for expansion and discovery, unencumbered by the relentless push to earn as much money as possible that may have entrapped you materially and spiritually in the second part of your life.

Your life will change dramatically from this point forward. Mexico is now your home, and you're on your way there. You will look back on the second part of your life with nostalgia, just as you look back on the first part of your life.

Most of the chapters in this part assume you will be driving. If you're flying, read the special instructions regarding documentation when flying in Chapter 2.

Chapter 1

Driving to the Border

You'll want to leave early in the morning if you want to minimize the number of nights spent in motels. Just pack your car, take your pets, take your cell phone, take a camera, lock the door, and go. Don't worry about what you might have forgotten, or forgotten to do. Just make sure your pets are comfortable, and then enjoy the ride and the scenery.

You're probably going to be driving through areas you've never seen before, so you'll want to take rest stops every few hours, not only for the obvious reasons, but also to admire the new area. On one of my rest breaks, I saw an Amish horse carriage moving at quite a fast clip-clop along the highway. Even though I had read about the Amish, and had seen them on TV, I was really amazed to actually see such an old-fashioned, black, covered carriage with a tall-hatted man driving it with reins. It was as if Abraham Lincoln had just driven by. I also saw Dollywood on another of my rest stops. It wasn't quite as inspirational, but fun, nevertheless.

Do keep in cell phone contact with a friend or relative along the way, especially if you're driving alone. You'll feel like you're sharing your adventure, and they'll be less worried about you.

Your Move: Driving to the Border

If the weather is warm, park in the shade and roll down the windows a few inches if you need to leave your pets in the car for a few minutes when you stop to get lunch. You can get your lunch to go, and eat outside with your dog on a leash, if the weather is nice.

If you've brought pets, it's good to know that all US Motel 6 motels always take them, because you'll find them everywhere. That said, Motel 6 motels are not all created equal. I found some to be surprisingly nice, and some were really not. Much depended upon how nice the town was, and how nice the particular area of the town was. All the rooms have access to the internet. Always take your laptop and your portable file folder containing your important papers and copies with you into your room overnight. If there's a store close by, get some apples, crackers, and string cheese for the next day's snacks.

"If you've brought pets, it's good to know that all US Motel 6 motels always take them, because you'll find them everywhere."

Also, if you plan to bring cats into your room to let them roam, make sure the room is cat-proofed first. If the base of the bed is not enclosed, the cats will have a place to hide where you will spend a long time swearing while trying to get them out. As a last resort, leave them in the car in their carrier with the windows rolled down ¼ of the way, unless it's very cold.

I found that eight hours was about the right amount of time to drive per day without getting groggy. I always had an early breakfast in a café or pancake house while the pets were still in the motel room. Then I'd drive (with one rest break) until noon or 1 o'clock for lunch. I'd have one or two rest breaks in the afternoon, and then drive until I found a highway sign for a Motel 6 around 5 o'clock, well before dark.

When you get to Laredo, Texas or whatever border town you've chosen, you'll notice that there are lots of *"Casa de Cambio"* stores or kiosks. That's where you'll want to exchange all your money into pesos. You won't be able to use US money anywhere along your drive to Lake Chapala—not for food, not for gas, and not for tolls. You will be able to use your Visa or MasterCard, though, at many of these places (not all)—that is, if your bank doesn't decline your Mexican transactions, even though you've called them in advance to alert them. If you get declined, call your bank again and complain. They should be able to fix the problem right away. But, you might as well get enough pesos for the whole trip. You'll need enough for your driver's fee, your driver's tip (10% is good), any motel costs, restaurants on the way, gasoline, tolls, and border crossing costs.

Your Move: Driving to the Border

Gasoline in Mexico costs about $4.00 USD per gallon (check bit.ly/2eP6pfl for current prices per liter). So, figure out how many miles your trip will be, divide that by how many miles per gallon your vehicle uses on the highway, and that's how many gallons you'll need. Multiply that times the cost in pesos per gallon (there are approximately 4 liters per gallon). That'll be your gasoline cost. The tolls will probably cost a total of 1000 pesos (about $56 USD). And, unless you end up paying import tax on something, your border crossing fees will probably be around $125 USD, plus, if you're importing a non-Mexican-plated vehicle, a vehicle deposit of between $200 USD and $400 USD (see the Index for more information on vehicle deposits).

"In Mexico, the dollar sign ($) is also used for pesos, which can be confusing."

By the way, in Mexico, the dollar sign ($) is also used for pesos, which can be confusing. In Mexico, sixty US dollars will look like this: $60 USD. Sixty pesos will look like this: $60 MXN or $60 MXP, or simply like this: $60. In most cases, common sense will tell you which is which, but be sure to ask, if you're not sure.

Chapter 2

At the Mexican Border

"If the border agents find even a half of a marijuana cigarette on you, you'll be in more trouble than you've ever imagined. Don't even think about it."

Whether you're driving or flying, it's very important not to attempt to cross the border with any illegal drugs, including marijuana, even in small amounts, and even if you come from a place where having small amounts is legal. This is also true for those who use marijuana for medical purposes. There's no such thing in Mexico. If the border agents find even a half of a marijuana cigarette on you, you'll be in more trouble than you've ever imagined. Don't even think about it. That goes for airplanes, too.

If you're driving, you'll want to cross the border first thing in the morning when you're fresh and ready for a full day. This is especially true if you have a border driver who is going to take you to your new home in one day without stopping anywhere overnight (yes, it's possible, but it takes about 12 hours).

The first thing I noticed when driving toward the Laredo border was that almost all the signs were only in Spanish. I

Your Move: At the Mexican Border

had been used to signs being in both English and Spanish in the US, but in Mexico (and even approaching Mexico, oddly), that's not the case. The second thing I noticed was that few of the border crossing staff spoke English. I suppose that's because most of them don't need higher education to do their jobs (like toll booth staff), but I was still surprised that they don't hire bilingual people there. Nevertheless, you'll get through it. Everybody does. Just smile, be cooperative, let them direct you, and be patient.

If you're coming from the US or Canada, you won't need a travel visa (not to be confused with a residence visa) to enter Mexico, but you might need one if you're coming from another country. Check this site for countries from which a travel visa is required: bit.ly/1Nt0hED.

Here are the things you will need to accomplish when crossing the Mexican border:

1. check in using an FMM form (see below)
2. if you're driving:
    a. get a temporary immigration vehicle permit (TIP), if you don't already have one and your vehicle has non-Mexican plates
    b. get Mexican car insurance, if you don't have any
3. pass through customs.

> *"It is very important to spell your name exactly as it appears on your passport, and that your middle name is not mistakenly used as your last name."*

For all the documents you will receive and sign, it is very important to spell your name exactly as it appears on your passport, and that your middle name is not mistakenly used as your last name.

FMM Form

If you are not a Mexican national (i.e., a Mexican citizen), you will need to fill out an FMM form. Here's a sample for people who have a pre-approved consulate visa:

Your Move: At the Mexican Border

If you're flying into Mexico, your airline staff will give you this form to fill out before landing.

This FMM form is sometimes referred to as the tourist form or the tourist card because it was used only to establish a status of Mexican Tourist before the new immigration law came into effect in 2012. Since then, it is used to track *all* entries and exits by foreigners.

If you are entering as a tourist (for up to 180 days), enter "Tourist" where it asks for immigration type (see item 8 on the sample form). If you have been pre-approved for a visa by your home country's Mexican consulate, you should indicate "Canje." If you already have a resident visa card (as you would on subsequent exits and entries, write either "Residente Temporal" or "Residente Permanente" there. Entering the correct status here is very important. If you mistakenly enter "Tourist" on item 8, that is what you will become, and it will be time consuming and expensive to undo later.

Show the immigration agent this FMM form so he or she can fill out the parts circled in yellow. If you have entered "Canje," you will have 30 days to *apply* for an actual residence visa card at your local Mexican immigration office. It may take some weeks to actually get your new card.

If you're driving, completion of the FMM form and issuance of the temporary vehicle permit is done in a government building away from the main traffic flow, so you'll want to take that exit as you approach the border. If you miss the exit (as I did), there are staff who will probably notice the lack of a temporary vehicle permit sticker on your car a little later, and they'll point you back to the right place. In my case, I still couldn't find the building, so one of the staff agreed to get in my car and navigate me there. That worked, but he asked for $200 pesos to get back out of the car. I thought that was a bit rich, so I gave him $50 pesos, instead, and said, "Adios." He grudgingly left. I smiled at him after he was out, and he smiled and waved back. I laughed it off, realizing that this may just be the way they earn a little extra for their efforts. I was grateful for the help.

It is in this building that you may want to meet your border driver, if you have one. Park in the building's parking lot, and bring your portable file folder with you inside. The people there do speak English.

You'll get your FMM form at the first window. You'll want to ask for the maximum time period of 180 days if you're a tourist. In any case, you will need your passport, a copy of your passport (face and signature page), and the FMM fee of 500 pesos (about $24 USD).

Vehicle Importation Permit and Deposit
After handing in your FMM form at the first window, if you're bringing in a foreign-plated vehicle, you'll be directed to another window to get your temporary vehicle

importation permit and sticker. They'll ask for your FMM form, your passport, your car's original title or your car's registration, driver's license, and various copies of these. If you don't have copies, there's another window just for making copies for a small fee. It's best to use your title, if you have it, since it shows ownership. That may come in handy if your vehicle is ever impounded.

You will get a temporary vehicle importation permit (called a TIP), which costs about $52 USD. The fee for a motor home or trailer is about $60 USD. Be careful to keep all your receipts. Otherwise, you may have to pay this again later.

If you're getting a temporary vehicle importation permit, you also have to pay a vehicle deposit. The deposit, which may be paid by cash or credit card, will be reimbursed when you take the car out of Mexico before the permit expires, or before the expiration of an extended date (if you get a residence visa) after properly notifying Aduana *(*customs*)*. The amount of your deposit depends on how old the vehicle is. For 2007 or newer vehicles, the amount is $400 USD. For 2001 through 2006 vehicles, it's $300 USD. For 2000 and older vehicles, it's $200 USD.

If you're a tourist, your temporary vehicle importation permit will be valid as long as you are allowed to stay, which is up to 180 days. If you have a Residente Temporal visa, the TIP is valid as long as it is.

The half sheet of colored paper your windshield sticker is on is your temporary vehicle importation permit (TIP). It is almost irreplaceable, and can cause you many problems if it is lost or stolen. Put a copy in your car's glove box, and keep the original in your file folder.

> *"The half sheet of colored paper your windshield sticker is on is your temporary vehicle importation permit (TIP). It is almost irreplaceable, and can cause you many problems if it is lost or stolen."*

If you already have a Residente Temporal visa card (not just a Canje from your home-country Mexican consulate), you can import your car permanently at the border, which is sometimes called "regularization" or "nationalization"—if your car qualifies. This process takes a few days at the border because a special customs broker is required, and because there are more steps. In all, the process costs about $1,500 USD or more. To qualify, the car needs to:

1. be between 8 and 9 years old (as of 2017, that means model years 2008 and 2009), or over 29 years old (classic)
2. have its VIN number (vehicle identification number) start with a 1, 2, 3, 4, or 5. That means it has been manufactured or assembled in a NAFTA country (US, Canada, or Mexico).

One customs broker in Nuevo Laredo and Laredo you could contact for more information is Grupo Cuevas at importaciondeautos.com.

Mexican Car Insurance

If you have applied for a temporary vehicle importation permit online, you will be required to purchase Mexican car insurance at that time. Otherwise, you can buy car insurance just before you leave the border building where you got your temporary vehicle importation permit. Sign up for the maximum coverage for 30 days. Make sure it covers bail bonds and legal expenses. It's very inexpensive. And, also make sure you know which drivers of your vehicle are insured. After you've moved in, you'll want to purchase annual car insurance at even better rates. Make sure you keep the business card in a secure place in your wallet. If you're in an accident in Mexico, calling your car insurance agent is one of the first things you'll want to do.

Just before you leave the parking lot, you'll see a booth where there are staff who will apply the vehicle permit sticker to your windshield in just the right place. If you miss the booth, you can apply the sticker yourself. It goes on the inside of the front windshield, in the center, just below your rearview mirror.

Customs

The customs area (Aduana) at the border is for making sure you don't have contraband, and for paying import duties on high-value items and new merchandise for sale. As you

Your Move: At the Mexican Border

approach the customs area, you'll see signs to move into different lanes if you have something to declare. That would be true if you're importing something you're planning to sell, or if you have something of particular value. If what you have in your vehicle are just normal household items, your own jewelry, art, electronics, and pets, you won't need to declare anything. So, you can just stay in the *"Nada que Declarar"* car lanes. You can check the following webpage to make sure that your items will be duty-free: bit.ly/2jiWKTh.

You'll see that every car in the normal flow of traffic will then get a green or a red stop light. If you get a green light (and ¾ of the time, you will), you've just cleared customs, and you're good to drive into Mexico. If you get a red light, you'll just pull over to the side, and follow the instructions of the customs officers. You may be asked to show your passport, the international health certificates for your pets, and answer various questions about where you're going, and why. They may ask you to remove various items for inspection, or not. In all cases, be pleasant and cooperative. You'll soon be on your way.

Chapter 3

Driving to Lake Chapala

At this point, your Mexican border driver, if you have one, will have taken over driving your car to Lake Chapala. Make sure everyone is wearing their seat belts; it's mandatory in Mexico.

One of the first things you'll notice (especially near the border) is that there will be guards, police, and sometimes Mexican military troops stationed at various points, and they'll have large rifles. You may even need to stop if there's a checkpoint. Do not become alarmed. They're there to prevent the transportation of illegal contraband—usually drugs going into the US, and weapons and ammunition going into Mexico. Just be cooperative and business-like.

"You'll want to take only toll roads (cuotas). They're very well maintained, and usually have four lanes."

This is the time to bring out your GPS, if you have one, so you can follow along on your route. If you want a map, they're usually sold at the gas stations along the way.

You'll want to take only toll roads (*cuotas*). They're very well maintained, and usually have four lanes. Non-toll roads (*libres*—free roads)

Your Move: Driving to Lake Chapala

are much less consistent because they get much less maintenance. They may be only two lanes wide with no shoulders, and they may have potholes. And, they're generally considered to be less safe.

There'll be toll booths on the toll roads, most of which (but not all) take MasterCard and Visa. The toll will be between 100 pesos and 300 pesos at each one, for a total of about between 700 and 900 pesos. Keep your toll receipts handy during your drive. Toll fees pay not only for general upkeep of the toll roads, but they also include insurance for you in case of an accident. It's very good insurance, too, paying for all costs, including all repairs and all medical bills.

> *"If you have an emergency while driving on the toll roads, call the **Green Angels (Los Angeles Verdes**), a fleet of radio dispatched trucks with bilingual crews. They can be reached by dialing **078 or 800-903-9200**."*

If you have an emergency while driving on the toll roads, call the **Green Angels (Los Angeles Verdes)**, a fleet of radio dispatched trucks with bilingual crews. They can be reached by dialing **078 or 800-903-9200**. Services include protection, medical first aid, mechanical aid for your car, and basic supplies. You will not be charged for services; only for parts, gas, and oil. Their services are paid for by the Mexican government. The Green Angels patrol daily from dawn until sunset, so try not to drive after that. If you are unable to call the Green Angels, pull off the road and lift the hood of your car. Chances are good they will find you. They come by frequently. Again, keep in mind that the toll you paid at the last toll booth includes insurance.

Part 4

Your First Few Weeks at Lake Chapala

Welcome—you're finally here! You will undoubtedly find that all your local Mexican and expat neighbors are friendly and helpful. Even if you live in a neighborhood that has mostly walled-in homes (a carry-over from Spanish hacienda and courtyard styles), as soon as you meet your neighbors (and you'll meet lots of people in the streets, stores, parks, and plazas), you'll be greeted warmly.

Although you'll enjoy meeting these new people, your best friends during your first months (aside from this book, of course) will probably be your landlord or agency staff. That's because they're the best ones to advise you about your initial utilities, food, water, and services. After your basic needs have been met, and you feel reasonably stable, you'll have more time for comparison shopping, new options, and your own explorations.

Chapter 1

Your First Week

Your first order of business, especially if you arrive at your home in the evening, is to make sure you'll be comfortable overnight, and that means water and toilet paper. Water straight from the tap is not clean enough to drink from unless you have verified that your house has a working water purification system. So, right after you open the front door of your new home, even before you tip your driver (about 10% of his fee) and send him on his way, head for the kitchen to see if there is any bottled water (you might arrange for that in advance). It will either be in the refrigerator, or in a stand-alone receptacle.

Next, go into the bathroom, and make sure there is toilet paper. If you've got water and toilet paper, you won't need to go back out until the morning. Otherwise, ask your driver to take you to the nearest 7-Eleven or OXXO store (it's like a 7-Eleven)—he'll know where they are—so you can get your essentials. Both of these stores never close.

By the way, the water is not so bad that you can't brush your teeth with it or wash your dishes with it. You'll ingest minimal amounts of water from those activities, and that won't give you any trouble. See the Index under Water for more information.

Your First Few Weeks at Lake Chapala: Your First Week

On your first full day, you'll probably want to go shopping for some basics to get you started. Because you'll need a broad range of items, the best place to go first is to Walmart. You'll find it similar to the Walmarts north of the border, but with somewhat fewer and different selections. Don't forget to add bottled water to your shopping list if your house doesn't have a water purification system. See the Index for Buying Groceries and for Buying Water for more information. If you don't have a GPS or a local map, don't be afraid to ask for directions. Everyone knows where the Walmart is. Just roll down your car window and ask, "*Donde está* Walmart, *por favor?*" (Where is Walmart, please?) This assumes, of course, that you have a vehicle to drive. If you don't, please see the Index for the chapter on Getting Around.

Walmart also has ATMs for Banamex and Bancomer, two of the most popular banks. This is a good place to withdraw cash (*efectivo*) from your debit or credit card. There'll be a fee (around $1.50 USD) if the card is not from Banamex or Bancomer.

Next, you'll want to call your real estate or rental agent or landlord to make an appointment with them. If you don't have a GPS or map, they can give you directions—or perhaps they can come to pick you up the first time. Take along a list of subjects you want to talk to them about, and then, do take notes because there will be lots of new information. Your list of subjects should include the following.

1. You'll want a list of **emergency numbers** for police, fire, and ambulance for your area. Compare them to the ones in the Appendix to make sure they're the most current.
2. If you don't have GPS, ask them if they have a local **map** you can keep.
3. Ask them if they will pay for changing all the **locks** because the previous residents (and their friends, relatives, and household staff) may have made and kept extra keys. If they won't pay for new locks, have it done anyway, and pay for it yourself. Ask them for a reference for this service because they may get a special discount.
4. If there's a **gardener** and/or **housekeeper** associated with your house, find out their names, whether they have their own keys, and what days and times they normally come. See the Index for more information about Housekeepers and Gardeners. You'll want to ensure that you're at home the first time they arrive in order to introduce yourself.
5. You'll want to know some information about your basic **utilities**. If you're renting, you'll already know from your lease whether your electricity, water, and gas are included in your monthly rent. If they're not, you'll want to make sure these accounts are transferred to your name, and that you won't be paying for the previous resident's expenses. You'll also want to know how and when you're expected to pay

your utility bills. Are they paid in person somewhere? If you're renting, are they paid through the agency? Whom should you call if there is a utility outage or emergency? What about on weekends? If it's the utility company itself, will there be English speakers available by phone? If you own your home, the seller or real estate agent can get all that information for you. No deposits are required for the utilities by the utility companies, but, if your landlord is going to pay them on your behalf, he/she may want you to keep a utility reserve account with him/her. See the Index for more information about Utilities.

6. You'll also want to know about your options for **TV**, **internet**, and land-line **phone**. Some of them may already be installed or available in your home. For instance, there may already be a particular vendor's roof-top satellite dish. That doesn't mean you have to sign up for that vendor, though. That's your decision to make. So, do ask your agency or landlord what's already installed. For more information about your choices, see the Index under Technology.

7. If you're renting, ask for a convenient time for them to conduct a **walk-through** of the house with you to write down any existing damage so it won't be deducted from your deposit when you leave. And then, make note of which of the damages you want fixed. For instance, if there's

a chip on a tile, you probably won't want to bother. You may be asked to contribute to or even pay for the costs if they are considered to be minor, and if you insist on having them fixed. Remember that in Mexico, landlords are only legally obligated to fix things that affect health and safety. However, the reputable rental agencies in the area are very much aware that renters from north of the border have somewhat higher expectations, and they try to be accommodating.

8. Ask for a good general **handyman** reference—someone who speaks some English (if you're not confident about your Spanish). Even though you may be the handy type yourself, there's a whole world of systems, contraptions, tools, and materials here that you've never had experience with before. Whether you own your home or you're renting, this will be an important contact person for you. Chances are that he (it's almost always a he) is already familiar with your home, and can give you excellent advice regarding upkeep and some of its quirks—and also give you advice about the best places to buy materials at low prices for your do-it-yourself projects later.

9. Ask about how much gas is left in your roof-top **gas tank**, how often it needs to be filled, and who to call to get it filled or looked at.

10. Also ask when the last time your roof-top **water tank** (*tinaco*) was cleaned out, and when the filter was last replaced. It's on your roof because gravity is what gives you your water pressure. Because the town water is not as clean as it is north of the border, sediment collects in the bottom of the tank and in the filter. Depending on which town you live in, you may need to have the tank cleaned every six months or every year, and the filter should be replaced every six months. If you rent, your landlord or rental agency usually pays for the tap water, so they will usually also pay for the *tinaco* maintenance. If not, check with your new handyman.

11. Similarly, you will need to have your ground-level water **cistern** (*aljibe*) cleaned out periodically, too. Unless you have a well, the cistern is where the town water enters your property and is initially stored. It has an electric pump that pumps water up to the roof-top *tinaco* when it runs low. This cistern needs to be cleaned out on the same schedule as the *tinaco*. So, you'll want to know when the last time was that it was cleaned out. If this is not cleaned out often enough, not only will you be washing your dishes with water that isn't as clean as it could be, but your laundry will start to show brown spots and not smell fresh. Your handyman should also be asked to put chlorine tablets in

the cistern (or you can do that yourself), but that should be in addition to, not a substitute for, the cleanings.
12. Find out about **garbage collection** in your neighborhood. How often is it collected, and when? Which materials are collected, and which are not? Where would you take the other materials? Are garbage cans required, or are just bags OK? Where should the garbage be placed— on the curb, or someplace else?
13. You'll also want to ask now about **fumigation/extermination** for insects (spiders, cockroaches, ants, scorpions). If you're renting, your landlord or agency may pay for that initially, or at least recommend a service that does that. In either case, you'll want to ask when the last fumigation was, and what the particular bug issues were. You can also buy cans of insecticide spray at Walmart or a hardware store (*ferretería*), of course.

Once you've set an appointment with your landlord or agency to discuss the above issues, you'll want to head for the **Lake Chapala Society**. It's located in Ajijic on a street called 16 de Septiembre (that's the date of Mexico's independence). The address is 16A. Their office and services are open from 10 to 2 Monday thru Saturday, and their grounds are open until 5. Call them at 376-766-1140 if you need directions. Or, you can visit their website at: lakechapalasociety.com. They're a wonderful non-profit

Your First Few Weeks at Lake Chapala: Your First Week

resource for all expats, and have a range of activities, information, courses, special interest groups, lending libraries, volunteer opportunities, and social events to keep you busy full-time, if you want. Plus, their grounds are beautiful: water-lily ponds, wandering egrets, lovely gardens, a gazebo, and plenty of patio furniture to just relax and have a snack at their cafe. They have a big community bulletin board, too, with notices of all kinds: home rentals and sales, pets for adoption, household help, items for sale, upcoming presentations on healthcare and immigration, and local events.

The first thing you'll want to do is head for the office there to learn about membership. Many of their activities and benefits are just for members, so most people do join.

After that, you might want to introduce yourself to the person in the information booth. That's an expat volunteer (almost everyone at the Lake Chapala Society is an expat volunteer) who has been in this area for at least two years, and can help answer any questions you may have about the area or services or special needs. They're there to help you—whether you're a member or not.

"The Lake Chapala Society could become like a second home to you."

The Lake Chapala Society could become like a second home to you. It is to many of Lake Chapala's expats. It's a friendly place to just connect with others like yourself—or to do nothing at all in a peaceful, supportive environment.

After that, you'll want to make extra house **keys**. This is particularly important if you have a walled-in back or side yard from which you can't get out unless you go through the house. The wind can easily slam the door shut and lock you out. So, keep a spare set of back or side door keys there so you never have to worry. That actually happened to me on a Sunday. I was lucky enough to have my cell phone with me, and the cell phone number of my handyman. Otherwise, I would have been stuck in my back yard for a very long time, not knowing how or who to call for help. You'll also want separate front door keys, garage keys, and car keys. And, you'll need a set of keys for your household help, as well, if they don't already have them.

There are many places to get keys made. But I recommend a particular locksmith and key store because they do a good job of filing down the metal burs, which can make the difference between the keys working smoothly or not—or not working at all—so you have to go back again to have them re-filed. It's a small yellow shack on the corner of Revolución and the *carretera* (the main road) in Ajijic. It's called *Cerrajería Cardenas* (Locksmith Cardenas), and it's located to the east side of the Bugambilias Plaza, right next to Salvador's Restaurant.

This first week at your new home is also a good time to make your **mailing services** choices. See the Index under

Mail for a full explanation. While you're near the Bugambilias Plaza getting your keys made, you'll also want to visit one of the three main mailing service stores in the area: Sol Y Luna (Sun and Moon) to ask about their services and rates. It's inside the Bugambilias Plaza. The entrance to the inside of the plaza is located in the front of the plaza (ask for directions at Salvador's Restaurant out in front—they're bilingual there). Sol y Luna is located all the way down inside the main entrance on the left. They're bilingual, too.

The above activities should keep you busy for the first week in your new home. In fact, many of these activities will keep you busy for a few weeks—maybe for a full month. You will find that they will take you longer than expected. That's because Mexico runs on Mexican time, as the saying goes—there's less of a sense of urgency here. Learn to relax, and try not to get frustrated. There's no need to hurry. Everything will get done soon enough.

Chapter 2

Your Second Week

By your second week, you'll have a fairly long to-do list left over from your first week, and you'll feel a little like a circus performer twirling plates on sticks. But there are several activities that are good to start in the second week. They'll take time to complete, too, but you'll be glad you started them now. In fact, there's no reason these couldn't be started in the first week. It's just that the activities listed for the first week are more important to start sooner.

If you received a visa sticker on your passport (approval to get a residence visa) from your home country's Mexican consulate, you have 30 days from when you crossed the border to *apply* to have it exchanged for your real **residence visa card**. Now is a good time to do that. Just visit the immigration office. (See the Index under INM.)

Another activity you will want to start now is to research your **health insurance** options. You will find that health care in Mexico is approximately 1/3 of the cost of similar care in the US. And yet, even at the reduced costs, a long-term serious illness or injury could still be financially devastating without some form of insurance. There are many options to choose from in Mexico. But be aware that there is usually a two-month coverage waiting period for private health insurance, so you will want to start this process now. And, do make sure that the health insurance you currently have is extended for at least that period of time in order to avoid any coverage gaps. See the Index under Health Insurance for more information.

One last activity you will want to start this week is to research your Mexican **cell phone** options. As you have probably determined, using your north-of-the-border cell phone in Mexico long term is expensive. Mexican cell phone services are much less expensive, especially since many do not require contracts. See the Index under Phones, Cell for more information.

Chapter 3

Your Third Week

Like the activities listed in the two previous chapters, the activities listed here can be done at any time, but are less urgent than the ones listed for the previous weeks. And, no doubt, you will still have a very full to-do list.

"Car insurance takes effect immediately upon signing up for it and paying for it, unlike health insurance, which has acceptance periods and waiting periods."

If you bought a 30-day Mexican **car insurance** policy at the border or online, it will expire next week. So, you will need to buy new car insurance this week—at a better rate. Car insurance takes effect immediately upon signing up for it and paying for it, unlike health insurance, which has acceptance periods and waiting periods. That's why you don't need to get a new policy before this week. You are required to buy car insurance by Mexican law and by Jalisco state law, and the consequences of not having it are quite severe. That is because in Mexico, being involved in a car accident is not a "civil" matter, as it is north of the border. It is considered a "criminal" matter because there is property damage and/or injury. As such, you can be jailed and your car can be impounded if you do not have the right protections. **Do not allow your car insurance to lapse.** It should include bail bond and legal expenses, and it is fairly inexpensive. It can also include towing service. It is the best money you can spend here in Mexico.

By this time, your new house is probably in need of cleaning. Do you want to do it yourself?

> *"Do not allow your car insurance to lapse...It is the best money you can spend here in Mexico."*

Consider the benefits of having a housekeeper. If your house doesn't already include a housekeeper, you can hire a woman (it's almost always a woman) to clean your whole house for very little money,

And, if your house doesn't already include a **gardener**, your lawn and garden might need some work, too, by this time. Gardeners are inexpensive, too, by north-of-the-border standards. But don't hire people who knock on your door looking for work, no matter how sorry you are to turn them away. These are people who will have access to your house, so you'll want to be as careful as you can about whom you choose. See the Index under Housekeepers and Gardeners for more information.

If you're interested in opening a Mexican **bank account**, now is a good time to begin that process. Many expats don't choose to open one, however; instead choosing to retain their home country bank accounts, and using those credit cards at Mexican ATMs. That works just fine, even long term, as long as you don't need to withdraw more money than your daily withdrawal limit allows. In that case, it helps to have more than one credit card. Most banks require you to have a residence visa to open an account, but not all. Bancomer is one that only requires a passport. See the Index under Banking for more information about your options.

Chapter 4

Whenever You Can

The activities listed in this chapter are dependent upon you having a residence visa (either a Residente Temporal or a Residente Permanente). If you entered Mexico as a tourist, none of the activities in this chapter apply to you. You can skip to Part 5—Living at Lake Chapala.

If you entered Mexico with a pre-approved visa sticker on your passport, you have 30 days to *apply* for a visa (whichever type you were approved for at your home country's Mexican consulate) at your INM office. When you have your visa card,

"By law, your car's importation permit status follows your immigration status."

which may take several weeks to be processed and printed, the following activities can be undertaken.

The first of these activities is to do a **vehicle importation permit notification** to Aduana (customs) to reflect your new visa status. The notification is not required by law, but you will lose your vehicle deposit when it expires otherwise. By law, your car's importation permit status follows your immigration status. So, when you get a residence visa, you no longer have to take your car across the border to re-apply for a temporary importation vehicle permit (TIP). Even though you will (eventually) have an expired temporary vehicle permit document, having your residence visa automatically means that your car's permit is valid, too. Some local police may try to give you a hard time for having an expired temporary importation vehicle permit. They may either not know the law very well in this regard, or they may just want to see whether they can extract a *mordida* (a little bite) from an unknowledgeable gringo. See the Index for more about *mordidas.* To prevent this, and to make sure you don't lose your temporary vehicle importation deposit, you will want to get an official letter from Aduana that states that your vehicle importation permit is valid. The best way to get that letter is to have a local immigration lawyer process it for you. One popular immigration lawyer locally is Spencer McMullen, Attorney and Official Court Translator. He can be reached at 376-765-7553. His website is ChapalaLaw.com.

When you have your extended vehicle importation permit letter, it's time to get **official certified copies** of your important documents. What this means is that you'll have copies of each of the documents that are certified to be as valid as the originals. Then you won't have to risk carrying around your originals, except in the case of your driver's license, of which you must always have the original when you're driving. The cost to get certified copies is very low, and can be done within half an hour. This requires a *Notario Público,* though. I can recommend Notaria 5 to you. That's located in the orange stucco building at 245-D Hidalgo (that's the *carretera*—the main road) in Chapala.

It's in the block just west of the main intersection of Hidalgo and Madero streets. They speak English, and are very easy to work with. The phone number is 376-765-2740.

By the way, a *Notaria Pública* is an office, and a *Notario Público* is a lawyer.

The documents you'll want certified to keep in your glove compartment are those that others might want to see when you're away from home. They include your:

- passport (the two pages with your photo and identification information)
- residence visa card (both sides)
- temporary vehicle importation permit (if you have a foreign-plated car)
- car registration (to show that your car's plates belong with that vehicle)
- letter from Aduana certifying that your tourist vehicle permit has been extended.

If you're over 60 years old, there are two discount cards that you're eligible for now that you have your residence visa. One is called **INAPAM**, and is the Mexican senior discount card. You'll get big savings (up to half off) on bus tickets, museums, airlines, and some restaurants. See the Index under INAPAM for more information. There's also a Jalisco state senior discount card referred to as **DIF**, which has similar savings. See the Index under DIF for more information.

Part 5

Living at Lake Chapala

This part of the book is meant to be used as an on-going reference.

Living at Lake Chapala, like living in any other part of Mexico, is not like living north of the border. You will quickly be reminded of all the government services that are taken for granted there (water purification, paved roads, regulations), and you will also see how rich your life can be without them. Life north of the border is more predictable, more efficient, more regulated, more automated, more expensive, and more bland. Looking back, it seems to me to be the vanilla version of life.

Life in Mexico, on the other hand, is a continuous adventure. It's colorful and surprising every day. Even for retirees, no two days are alike. There's much more life on the streets, the plazas, and the parks. There are people still riding horseback on the streets here as their primary mode of transportation. There are impromptu fruit and food stands everywhere. The children are generally happier than I've seen north of the border, running around in the neighborhoods like we did in the US in the 50s and the 60s. It's a place where people really interact, and real relationships form.

But it's not perfect here—not even the weather, contrary to what you may have heard or read. The Lake Chapala area's climate is said to be semi-tropical and perennially spring.

It is sunny almost every day, and the average annual temperature is 67.8°F, but that includes night as well as day, and it includes all the seasons. The real temperatures swing quite a bit from that average. For instance, the hottest time of the year is in April, May, and June, when the daytime temperatures reach into the 80s and 90s every day, and the night temperatures are in the mid to upper 60s. It's then that you'll wish you had air conditioning, even though the air is dry. After the rainy season comes in mid-June, bringing rain frequently at night, the daytime temperatures drop to the upper 70s and 80s during the day and the mid 60s at night, but the humidity is higher. The rainy season lasts until around the end of September, when the temperatures and the humidity gradually decrease until December and January, when the daytime temperatures are between the 50s and 70s, and the night temperatures drop to the low 40s. Then you'll wish you had a heater.

Houses here are generally not equipped with either air conditioners or heaters, but most people do have fans and portable heaters for the extremes. All things considered, the climate here is probably as close to perfect as you're likely to find anywhere—especially, as perfect as you're likely to find anywhere you can afford to live.

In almost all other regards, you'll discover that there are challenges here every day—challenges that will stretch you, make you laugh, surprise you, frustrate you, teach you, and ultimately—make you feel alive.

Chapter 1

Legal Basics

This chapter cannot delve into all the legal system differences between Mexico and north of the border, of course, but there are a few legal basics (some surprising) that are very important for all expats to know. That's why this chapter is listed first.

Mexican lawyers are called *abogados* (or *licenciados*). They can be licensed by individual states, or they can be licensed by Mexico, which means they can practice in all states. Most of them speak English.

A second type of lawyer is called a *Corredor Publico*. This type of lawyer specializes in commerce issues, such as setting up corporations and filing insurance documents. There are very few of these Lakeside. You'll want to look in Guadalajara for one, or simply use a *Notario Público* (the next level up), instead.

A Mexican *Notario Público* is not at all like Notary Publics north of the border. They can be appointed by a Mexican state or by the federal district of Mexico City, or by passing a difficult application and examination process, and then undergoing many years of apprenticeship. This is a highly regarded position, therefore. *Notarios Públicos* are the only ones authorized to prepare real estate transfer documents, mortgages, wills, and to certify documents.

All vehicle accidents are considered criminal rather than civil events, since property has been damaged and/or people have been hurt.

Mexico's criminal legal system is based upon Napoleonic Code. That is, you are considered guilty until proven innocent. There has to be some reasonable evidence, of course, that you were involved (the police don't just randomly accuse people of crimes, and then force them to prove their innocence). What it does mean is that you can be arrested and detained at the scene for being involved in an accident regardless of whose fault it is. The process of fault determination may take weeks, months, or more, depending on the complexity of the accident. Your car can be impounded, as well. For these reasons, it's good to have a local lawyer (*abogado*) you can call right away to protect you. Here is one:

> *"Mexico's criminal legal system is based upon Napoleonic Code. That is, you are considered guilty until proven innocent."*

Lic. Spencer McMullen
(045) 331-556-0828
Attorney and official court translator

By the way, make sure any lawyer you choose is authorized to practice law before the courts. Some call themselves lawyers without actual credentials. The only way to make sure is to ask to see their *cédula* (official certificate), and to make sure it's current.

All legal documents must be signed in blue ink exactly as you signed your passport. Copies of all documents should be black and white only. Color copies are suspected be attempts to forge documents.

Non-Mexicans are prohibited from participating in Mexican politics. You can discuss politics in private or in small groups, but you can't participate in public protests, sign petitions, or support any politician or party. This is a deportable offense.

The defamation laws against libel (written) and slander (oral) in Mexico used to be very strict. A law was passed in 2007, however, that de-criminalizes them. Until then, the news media were constantly being threatened by defamation suits in order to prevent them from writing negative information, even if true. Now there is only the possibility of a fine, and the possibility of a civil suit if it's a serious enough case, and if a judge chooses to undertake it. There are no jury trials here, and oral trials have only just been instituted.

There are not as many civil suits in Mexico as in the US, for a number of reasons. They're very expensive, there are no punitive damage awards, and the amount of time for the suit to be resolved is long. Informal and out-of-court settlements are the best options in Mexico.

Having unauthorized drugs, weapons, or ammunition in Mexico is extremely serious, except having small amounts of recreational marijuana (bringing any amount across the border in either direction is very serious, however). Most drugs and weapons offenses carry significant jail terms. It can also take up to a year to have your case heard, during which time you may be waiting in a Mexican jail, which is not known for comfort.

Chapter 2

The Towns

The Lake Chapala area is made up of small towns and villages—not cities. This is important when considering what you will find there, and what you won't. Although a Walmart store has opened here, there are no other "big box" stores or malls to speak of - yet. There's no McDonald's, either. Most people consider this a good thing until they want to buy something above and beyond everyday needs, or when a Big Mac attack hits. Then they have to go to Guadalajara.

Each town has its own character, as you might expect, and even several characters since many of them have the old traditional area of town, and then a slightly built-up area that's a little more modern. Some towns have gated communities now, complete with condo fees, that are every bit as modern as north of the border.

All of the towns have a few features in common. They have cobblestones on their streets (except on major roads) which were originally laid during the days of Spanish rule in the 16th century. The cobblestones are not even-sized, manufactured cobblestone bricks or pavers. They're real, uneven, mostly rounded stones—sometimes quite large. They're not easy to walk on, especially for people with balance problems. They are, however, easy and inexpensive to maintain, they keep the traffic from going fast, and they don't really damage cars that have decent shock absorbers and tires. Many places also have speed bumps (*topes*) that reduce speed even further in some busy areas, eliminating the need for a lot of (costly) traffic lights.

Also, you'll notice that many of the houses, especially in the older parts of town, can't be seen because they're surrounded by walls. This is a carryover from the old Spanish haciendas with their beautiful courtyards. The outside may look narrow and rustic, but the entire inside of the block is a paradise of flowers and patios. The tradition of the walls has been kept up over time because houses with no walls by contrast look more accessible to burglars. And no one wants to stand out as having the most accessible house in the neighborhood. So the custom continues. That changes as new neighborhoods are built, however. In newer developments, fewer of the houses have security walls, and front lawns are landscaped in order to open up the view.

Another thing most of the towns have in common is a plaza, sometimes with a central gazebo. It's like a town square where people gather in an open area to sit on benches, sometimes listen to speeches and music, chat with their neighbors, and enjoy a respite in the open air.

There are towns all around Lake Chapala. But the center of the expat community is on the north shore of the lake— from Chapala on the east to Jocotepec on the west. The farther away from the north shore you get at Lake Chapala, the fewer expats there will be, and the less English will be spoken. Some expats do choose to live on the south shore and love it, after they feel comfortable living in more rustic areas without the support of other expats close by, and after they have learned enough Spanish to communicate well. But, this book is a guide for newcomers, so I will only recommend the north shore for the first six months in this area.

In looking at a map of the north shore, you'll see a road running all the way through the towns. This is called the *carretera* (main road, or highway). Each town has a different official name for it. In Chapala, it's called Hidalgo. In some parts of San Antonio Tlayacapan, it's called Calle Chula Vista, and in the La Floresta area, it's called both Boulevard Oriente Jin Xi (named after a Chinese immigrant) and Avenida Luis Donaldo Colosio. And in Ajijic and west of there, it's named either the Carretera Ote., which is short for *oeste* (west), or Carretera Pte., which is short for *poniente,* which also means west. But, it's the same road.

The area to the south of this highway is called the lake side or "lower," as in Lower San Antonio. The area to the north is called "upper," as in Upper Ajijic. The upper parts of the towns tend to be a little more expensive because their views are better, and because they get better breezes. More expats tend to live there. There are some breezes close to the lake, of course, but they tend to get blocked by the walled houses there. Most new development is built in the upper areas not only for that reason, but also because that's the only direction expansion can go. There is no real advantage in living closer to the lake as there is in most communities north of the border because the lake coastline is mostly undeveloped. Real estate prices are not much higher there, if at all, for that reason. There are no sand beaches, and no grass, except in the parks. There are beautiful palm-tree-lined boardwalks (*malecónes*), however, and quite a few charming restaurants along the coastline in some of the towns.

Ajijic

The epicenter of the expat community is Lower Ajijic (pronounced ah-hee-HEEK) in *El Centro* (downtown). You'll sometimes see it spelled Axixic (pronounced the same way), which is the indigenous spelling. Ajijic is home to the Lake Chapala Society (including the largest English-language library in Mexico), many wonderful hotels and bed-and-breakfast inns, lots of fabulous restaurants, live music of all sorts, and many wonderful art galleries, art shops, clothing stores, and boutiques. Aside from all these exciting shops and activities are a beautiful, long, palm-lined *malecón,* a large restaurant-lined plaza, and a large Catholic church—San Andrés—which was founded in the 16th century, and rebuilt in the 18th century. Surprisingly, all the shops and restaurants are intermingled with walled-in residences, many of which have live roosters. Zoning laws seem to be non-existent. This is both good and bad. It's an easy walk to everything, and you feel as if you're in the middle of everything. But you also get the noise, the construction sites, the cooking odors, and the nightclub music. And, when the snowbird tourists arrive from October to April, you get the most tourists, too. That means traffic build-ups, and much less available parking.

> *"The farther away from Ajijic you go in either direction, the lower the prices will be— real estate prices, rentals, and everything else."*

The streets in *El Centro* Ajijic are narrow, so many of them are one-way and only allow parking on one side of the street. West Ajijic has wider streets and larger houses that are not so close together. But all of Ajijic maintains its old customs and a slow pace of life, and is very popular. Both Lower and Upper Ajijic are somewhat pricey compared to other towns simply because they're the center of everything. In fact, the farther away from Ajijic you go in either direction, the lower the prices will be—real estate prices, rentals, and everything else.

There are some less rustic, newer *colonias* (neighborhoods) along the edges of Ajijic that you might want to explore. The houses are further apart from each other, there's more grass, and a more north-of-the-border, open feel. Some of them are quite suburban. On the east side near Walmart there is La Floresta (where you can also rent horses), and there are many new gated and ungated neighborhoods all along the upper edges of Upper Ajijic that you can easily find on a map.

San Antonio Tlayacapan

To the east of Ajijic is the town of San Antonio, as most people refer to it. The streets are more residential, less compacted, and less "artsy" than in Ajijic. As with most of Lower Ajijic, Lower San Antonio has traditional, rustic house styles. And, it has a typical small-town Mexico feel, too. There's a plaza and small mom and pop stores (*tiendas*). There's also a *colonia* in Lower San Antonio called Mirasol, which has more modern houses with lawns. Upper San Antonio has quite a few more modern *colonias*, like Chula Vista (which has a golf course), along the Libramiento. The Libramiento is a highway (non-toll, or free) that intersects the main *carretera* across from Walmart in San Antonio. The other end of the Libramiento merges with Highway 23, which connects Chapala with Guadalajara. It was built to provide a shortcut from Guadalajara to the western towns without going through Chapala.

Chapala

Chapala is the biggest town at Lakeside. The central part of Chapala (*El Centro*) does not have as high a ratio of expats to locals as most of the western towns. It's very traditionally Mexican, with a large church, a big plaza, and a *mercado* (a covered, on-going market area). It also has big parks. These are great places to take your dogs. There are no pet restrictions in the parks. I've even seen horses and cows grazing in Cristiania Park. Chapala also has wonderful lakeside features, like a big *malecón* (boardwalk), a large sculpture fountain, and lots of restaurants.

This is where Guadalajarans come for weekend get-aways, so there's quite a bit of additional traffic in *El Centro* Chapala then, as well as on festival days (which are often). Then there's *banda* music, mariachi bands, fireworks, and parties. So, this is where the non-expat action is. The houses and neighborhoods are traditionally Mexican, too, and get increasingly modern at the perimeters where the newer developments are. There are a few suburbs to the north, like Chapala Heights, and to the east, like Vista del Lago, too.

Everything costs less in Chapala than in the western towns because it's priced more for Mexicans than for expats. So, unless proximity to particular stores is a high priority for you, you'll stretch your pesos farther by shopping in Chapala for everything, including housing. There are more small towns east of Chapala on the north shore of the lake, but I don't recommend them for newcomers because there's not as much expat support there, including the use of English.

> *"Everything costs less in Chapala than in the western towns because it's priced more for Mexicans than for expats."*

San Juan Cosalá

There are lots of small subdivisions along the *carretera* west of Ajijic. They're quite often of mixed character—traditional and modern (more traditional on the lake side). The next sizable town to the west of Ajijic is San Juan Cosalá, which, right along the *carretera*, is very traditional. Whereas most of the other towns and neighborhoods along the lakeshore are a little set back from the *carretera*, in San Juan Cosalá, you will see a great deal of life because there are houses and small stores and people milling around very close to the *carretera*. It is a very poor town, however.

Just before you get to the residential area, there's a stretch of tourist restaurants all along the highway overlooking the lake, which has a tendency of slowing the flow of traffic because it has many *topes* (speed bumps), but it's entertaining, nevertheless, as parking attendants frantically flag down prospective customers to the parking areas.

The biggest modern development in Upper San Juan Cosalá is the Raquet Club, which has a high percentage of expats, and has its own sports club and beautiful views of the mountains and the lake.

Jocotepec

As you drive west of San Juan Cosalá, you'll notice that there's a fork that goes north to connect to Highway 15, which runs north (to Guadalajara) and south (around the lake). But the main *carretera* dips south through Jocotepec, the western-most town on the north shore of Lake Chapala.

This is one of the oldest towns in the area, having been found by the Spanish in 1528. It has a sizeable *El Centro* area, and a beautiful *malecón* (boardwalk). It's about the size of Ajijic, but it has fewer expats, so far. Most of the town has a very traditional character, with newer developments being built around the edges. The cost of living there is about the same as in Chapala—prices reflecting a Mexican, rather than an expat, budget.

Municipalities

All the towns mentioned above fall within two municipalities (counties), which control the various governmental agencies (fire department, police department). The municipality of Chapala includes all the towns and villages east of San Juan Cosalá (including Ajijic). The municipality of Jocotepec includes San Juan Cosalá, and all the towns and villages west. It is much more Mexican in flavor, generally, and housing is much cheaper.

Chapter 3

Language and Social Customs

Some guidebooks will tell you that you don't need to speak Spanish to live at Lakeside because everyone understands and speaks at least a little English because of all the expats. The first part of that sentence is correct: you don't have to be able to speak Spanish in order to get along here. But it's not true that most of the Mexicans here speak English, or even understand it. These are small towns filled with small-town people whose culture has deep roots. They're not as cosmopolitan or highly educated as people are in Guadalajara, for instance, where more business is conducted in English. Unless you plan to live completely closed off from your surroundings, you will want to know more about the people you've chosen to live among. And that means learning their language and customs. You will be amazed at how much you will learn about Mexicans and their culture just by picking up a little language.

Language

The way to get along at Lakeside without knowing Spanish is to rely on your rental or real estate agents, the volunteers at the Lake Chapala Society, your fellow expats, and the Mexican people you'll meet who do know English. And when none of them are around, you'll learn to play charades. When I wanted to buy mosquito repellent at Farmácia Guadalajara soon after I arrived, I had to simulate a mosquito flying around and then landing on and biting my arm. To my chagrin, I learned that the Spanish word for repellent is *repelente*. So, it can be done, but you'll probably feel foolish and dependent.

Remember when you lived north of the border, and people got frustrated with those who spoke the wrong language? Now that's you. You're holding up the checkout line because you don't understand what the cashier is saying, you can't telephone customer service for your TV service outage because no one there speaks English, you can't read the words on food or product containers, and you wouldn't know what to say if you had to call the fire department. So, what to do? Below are some activities to begin as soon as possible.

> *"Remember when you lived north of the border, and people got frustrated with those who spoke the wrong language? Now that's you."*

If you haven't already done so, the first activity is to learn to count in Spanish, including all the hundreds, as mentioned in Part 2—Before Your Move. You'll need to be able to understand and to say numbers for everything you spend money on—which will be a lot when you first arrive.

Make flash cards and test yourself until you're sure you know them. And, make sure you can identify them as they're being spoken. Mexicans tend to speak quickly. Not only will you need to know your numbers, you will need to

140

be able to identify and count money. So, as soon as you get some Mexican pesos, take some time to study all the bills and coins so you're confident you can identify them when you're in a store under a little pressure. You'll be thankful you put in the study time because paying money and getting change will constitute the majority of your conversations with Mexicans at first.

The second activity, which you should do before leaving your home country, actually, is to buy books. One is Madrigal's Magic Key to Spanish by Margarita Madrigal. It's a step-by-step beginning Spanish course, and it's very good (private tutors here often use it). By the time you get to chapter 10, though, you will realize that you need someone to answer questions. But as a self-study book on Spanish, if you have the discipline to persevere on your own, this is excellent. The drawback is, of course, that you never get to speak or hear, or put your own sentences together. The second book is 501 Spanish Verbs by Barron's (also used by tutors here), and it's an excellent reference on Spanish verbs and their conjugations, which may be the most difficult aspects of Spanish to learn. You can find these books on Amazon, eBay, and locally.

The third activity you can do before leaving your home country is to install some language translation applications on your smartphone or tablet, if you have one. The first app is **Google Translate**, and it's free. It translates words between 90 languages. You can either type the word or speak it, and it will pronounce the word for you, too. It's very handy, but it does require internet access. It now includes a formerly independent application called Word Lens, though, which does not require internet access. If you hold up your device's camera lens to a sign or document, it will translate the words on it in real time. It's quite amazing to see. Another of its functionality is a straight-forward word translation, whereby you type in a word, and it will give you all the different meanings. Word Lens does not require an internet connection, so you can use it anywhere. I've used it for menus, signs at the park, contracts, and my Mexican cell phone instruction manual.

Soon, you're going to want to actually speak Spanish, though. I was intimidated by the language at first. When I was in the United States, I heard Spanish fleetingly on Spanish TV channels, and I thought it sounded like machine-gun fire. The rapid delivery and the rhythm of the language made me think it was almost impenetrable. But as soon as I started recognizing a few words, the mysteries of the language started to reveal themselves. I have three recommendations for you, all of which can be done simultaneously, if you have the time and energy.

Learning a new language does take time and effort—probably more than you anticipate. If you're not studying it an hour a day, the new language just won't sink in and stay there. That's been my experience. So, it's a commitment—one that you probably won't have adequate time and attention for until you begin your second month at

Lakeside. Your first month will be hectic enough. But you can certainly get ready and plan for these activities now.

The first activity is to sign up for the next Spanish 1A class at the Lake Chapala Society (see bit.ly/2vQjrjD). It costs 750 pesos (about $42) plus a workbook and a set of flashcards. The course is based on the Warren Hardy method, is 7 weeks long with a two week break, and then you start the next course (1B). You'll be speaking some useable sentences within just a few weeks, and you'll gain confidence as you go. You'll be in a class twice a week for 1-1/2 hours each, with a bilingual instructor and up to 7 other students (usually less). It's a great way to get started, and to feel the support of your class, who will be struggling along with you. It's a very non-threatening atmosphere, but you do have to work in class and at home. It isn't easy, but it is worthwhile.

Another popular option for group Spanish classes is Olé México (766-2068, olemexico.mx), located in Ajijic at Revolución #6. The classes are small (5 people or less), and are not based on the Warren Hardy method. Grammar and conversation are taught simultaneously. There are four general levels of Spanish instruction, starting with beginners. An initial consultation will determine which level you are ready for, and the first actual class is free. Students have a choice of days of the week and times of the day. The fees are about $70 USD per month for twice-per-week classes of 1-3/4 hours each. Or, a student can choose a three-times-per-week schedule for about $90

USD per month. Modern teaching methods are used throughout, including the use of their own creative word exercises and activities, games, and stories to listen to, to read, and to invent. A great deal of personal interaction and personal attention to progress is offered in a very cheerful, patient, non-threatening, and enjoyable, well-controlled setting. White boards are used extensively to illustrate words and concepts. The instructors only speak English in class when they have to. By the second level, the instructors speak only Spanish in class. I have taken these classes, myself, and I recommend them highly. They also provide private lessons for about $8.00 USD per hour.

Social Customs

One of the best ways to be accepted by your new Mexican community is to participate in their social customs.

For instance, meeting other adults, even just passing a stranger on a sidewalk, calls for a respectful acknowledgement and greeting. Always wish them *"buenos dias"* if it's before noon, *"buenas tardes"* if it's between noon and 7pm, and *"buenas noches"* if it's after 7pm—regardless of when it gets dark. You'll always get a smile and a similar return greeting. For children, a more casual *"hola"* (oh-la) will do. Upon leaving, a simple *"adiós"* is fine, which will be responded to with either *"adiós"* or *"que le vaya bien,"* which roughly translated means "may it go well with you."

When someone sneezes, you'll want to say "*salud*" instead of "bless you." It means "health."

When you need to pass or get by someone, the correct expression is "*con permiso, por favor.*" That means "with your permission, please." You are asking for their space. They will reply "*pase,*" meaning "pass," or "*propio,*" meaning "you own it." They have given up their space.

If you accidentally bump into someone, you should say, "*perdón*" (pardon). If you need someone's attention, you should say "*disculpe*" (excuse me). In English, we usually say "pardon" in all three cases, but in Mexico, there's a distinction.

Also unlike north of the border, you need to excuse yourself if you leave a group, just as you would excuse yourself when leaving a meal. You shouldn't just turn and leave. You should say "*Con permiso, por favor.*"

These may seem like minor courtesies, but they're very important to Mexicans, and they show that you have good manners.

Speaking of space, I have read somewhere that Mexicans' need for personal space is much less, so they end up standing closer to us northerners than we are comfortable with. I have not found that to be the case. It seems to me to be exactly the same.

I had also heard that women should never make direct eye contact with, or smile at, Mexican men they don't know—that it's interpreted as being inviting. I have not found that to be the case, either. That may have something to do with my age, but I don't think so. I have found Mexican men to be unfailingly polite and respectful to women.

> *"Your waiter will never give you the check until you ask for it."*

Another courtesy many Mexicans observe is to wish other diners *"Buen provecho"* (I hope you get the most from your meal) when leaving a restaurant. The diners will look up and say *"Gracias."* Saying it just once (not to every diner) is fine.

Another custom in restaurants is that your waiter will never give you the check until you ask for it. It's considered rude, as if implying that you should pay and leave now. The correct way to ask for the check is *"La cuenta, por favor."*

When you want to get a waiter's attention, never call out "waiter." It's considered impolite to be hailed by your profession, just as it would be if you were to call out "cleaning lady." Use *"disculpe"* or *"señor"* or *"señorita,"* instead.

Also, to Mexicans, it's considered poor form to suggest going "Dutch"—each paying for his own meal. It's considered an honor to pay for a friend's or a group's meal, and it will most likely be reciprocated at another time. However, if the tab is agreed to be split, it's always split evenly—even if one person just has a drink, and another has a seven course meal. To be clear, this is true for Mexican culture, but between expats, whatever is agreed upon is fine. Waiters know that foreigners sometimes only pay for their own meals.

And lastly, regarding tipping, 10% to 15% in restaurants is fine. 20% is going overboard. Don't be tempted to buy respect by over-tipping. Mexicans view tips as tokens of courtesy only, not as pay-offs.

"Whoever makes the invitation to dine should pick up the whole tab, especially if it's a gathering."

Negotiating Prices

First, there are certain places where negotiating is acceptable, and places where it isn't. For restaurants and grocery stores and for daily staples, no. But for general merchandise, such as clothes and furniture and art purchased from individuals or thrift stores, or anywhere out in the open, yes. For housing (even rentals), sometimes. For cars and large-ticket items, yes. For services, like construction quotes, yes. But, approach negotiating carefully and respectfully, even if you suspect that the price you've been quoted is a "gringo" price (higher than normal because you can probably afford it). Negotiation is a subtle art, one that Mexicans are good at with each other since they've had lots of practice. Expats (to over-generalize) tend to be ham-handed. The Donald Trump approach won't work here. I've heard from Mexicans that some expats start by offering a price that is so low as to be offensive.

> *"I've heard from Mexicans that some expats start off by offering a price that is so low as to be offensive. Mexicans will often simply refuse to negotiate after that because they've been dishonored."*

Mexicans will simply refuse to negotiate after that because they've been dishonored. Don't start your bid at less than half the original price. You'll have better success by starting at a discount of 25%. Offer a reasonable price. Don't make it a contest.

Negotiating is sometimes best accomplished by having a Mexican person negotiate on your behalf, as an expat I know does. He has a Mexican housekeeper whom he sends out to buy things for him. She gets the "Mexican" prices, and is good at getting the lowest price possible while still maintaining the honor of the seller. You may not have a Mexican personal shopper since you're a newcomer, of course. But it's an interesting idea to keep in mind.

Chapter 4

Getting Around

There are many options for getting around on the north shore of Lake Chapala. The towns were established centuries ago when people either walked or rode a horse or a mule. So the streets, especially in the centers of the towns, are narrow, and the blocks aren't long. Although some Mexicans still ride horses through the streets, walking is the best way to see each town to see life as it's really lived. Although the streets are cobblestoned, the sidewalks are usually better for walking, although they're often narrow and slanted.

What requires some extra thought is traveling between the towns. The most obvious solution is to drive your own car. But it isn't the only solution because many people don't own cars here, and many like it that way.

Rental Cars

During your initial exploratory trip to the area, you will want to consider renting a car (*coche* or *carro*) so you can explore the different towns and neighborhoods efficiently. Later, if you don't have your own car, visiting guests might like to drive around to different areas, too. There is a car rental agencies in the area that has a good reputations (there may be others, too). It's Línea Profesional, and it's located between Madero and Guerra streets on the north side of the *carretera* in Ajijic. For more information, see bit.ly/2wVThii. It pays to make reservations in advance because they have a smaller inventory of cars than at the airport, for instance, and because the days and hours they're open may not be consistent.

> *"Many people will reserve a rental car online, and arrive to find that the rental price they thought they got was only a part of the cost."*

You'll want to be very careful about costs. Many people will reserve a rental car online, and arrive to find that the rental price they thought they got was only a part of the cost. Be sure to ask about the insurance cost up front. There will probably be a mandatory daily insurance cost. Often this insurance is tiered. For example, they will tell you that they will require a $10,000 USD hold on your credit card for, say, a $20 USD extra daily payment, but to bring that deposit down to a more realistic $1,200 hold deposit, it will cost you something like $50 extra per day. The actual car rental cost itself is very inexpensive—between $14 and $20 per day—but most people mistakenly think this is all they have to pay. The annual cost of car insurance in Mexico may be cheap, but daily, weekly, even monthly car insurance is very expensive.

You will want to consider renting a golf cart, instead. One such rental place is lakechapalagolfcarts.com.

Taxis

Taxi drivers in this area usually know at least a little English. Many have spent time in the US saving enough money to buy into the market here so they can have a career to support their families and to be with them. There are taxi stands where you'll see the yellow taxis waiting for fares. These are in the major tourist areas, such as at the big plazas, and they're called "*sitios*" (on site). The *sitios* are preferable to the free-lancers (who don't have "*sitio*" printed on the cars) since *sitios* are licensed by the government.

You'll find taxis to be inexpensive by north of the border standards—so much so that some people use taxis (and buses) instead of having cars. They say that the cost per month is about the same—without the hassle of having to buy or sell a car, or of having breakdowns and repair bills, or of having to get licenses and permits. If you need taxi services after 5pm, though, it's best to make prior arrangements, since their normal hours are during daylight.

Do ask for a rate quote before you begin your trip so there'll be no last minute surprises. And do tip your driver 10% - 15% of the fare. The phone numbers for the main *sitios* in the area are listed in the Appendix. You can also search the area's web boards (also listed in the Appendix) for recommendations for particular drivers.

Uber

Although Uber (the taxi alternative, with locals driving their own cars) hasn't yet been officially approved in the Lake Chapala area, their cars are already here and ready for service. That's because Uber has been approved by Guadalajara and the airport, so they do come here. There are probably around five cars at any one time, and their services cost less than taxis. To register, be sure to list your home city as Guadalajara (your full address will not be required). You will not be able to register if you list your home city as one of the towns in the Lake Chapala region (for now).

Hiring a Driver

There are people in this area, usually men, who are hired as personal drivers, either part time or full time. They're usually taxi drivers, so this arrangement is generally just a matter of finding a taxi driver you like and trust, and negotiating your requirements. Some people hire drivers to go to the US border, for instance, or to go to the airport or to go shopping in Guadalajara, or to be a tour guide there for the day. Others pay just to have someone available to drive at any time or for appointments.

Local Buses

The local bus system is very reliable, low-cost, and safe. Most of the Mexican locals who do not have cars use buses to go everywhere. There are full-size buses that travel the length of the *carretera* from Jocotepec to Chapala every 20 to 30 minutes. They start at about 6am and go until about

9:30pm. Some may start a little earlier or run until a little later, and on weekends and holidays, the schedule is less precise. But, be aware that some of them bypass Chapala going east, taking the Libramiento shortcut to Guadalajara, instead. So, if your destination is Chapala, you'll want to make sure that the sign at the front of the bus says Chapala— or ask the driver if he or she goes to Chapala.

There are also smaller buses that are about ¾ the size of full-sized ones. These also run along the *carretera* from Chapala. But these buses loop through the side streets of two of the towns: San Antonio and Ajijic. And they don't go further west than Ajijic. You'll want to refer to the Mexico Travelers Map Guide for the exact routes, or just ride one for the complete loop to see how close it gets to where you want to go. They usually run between 7am and 8:30pm at 15 minute intervals. One senior has told me that she likes these smaller buses better because the straps and handles for holding on are better. This could be important if you have balance problems because some of the drivers are quite adventurous going around corners.

The fares for buses depend on where you're getting on and where you're getting off, of course, but in general, the fare is around 10 pesos. Only cash is accepted, so do bring coins for change or small bills. If you have a DIF senior discount card (see the Index for DIF cards), your fare will be cut in half. Hardly anyone does this for short rides, though. When you get on, tell the driver where you're going—the town and the street or landmark, if possible, and he'll tell you what the fare is. When you want to get off, push the red button on the pole near the back of the bus for the bus stop. Or, go to the front of the bus, and indicate to the driver when you want to get off.

"If you have a DIF senior discount card (see the Index for DIF cards), your fare will be cut in half."

Bus stops are not always marked. The places where there are covered benches are a good bet, though, as are places where others are waiting. In general, bus drivers will pick you up if you flag them down anywhere along their route—especially near a local attraction or corner.

Tours

During the first few months of your stay at Lake Chapala, you'll probably be too busy to go on any extended travel tours. If you do want to take a tour out of the area, though, you'll be pleased to know that the big tour buses (sometimes called first-class buses) are excellent. They're ideal for long-distance travel, being outfitted with air-conditioning, bathrooms, foot rests, very cushy seating, and sometimes even TVs and videos. They also have bins for luggage above the seats, as well as in the bottom cargo area. Some of these buses run through the Lakeside area into Guadalajara. Those have higher fares, and can be paid for right on the buses.

For real tours, though, you have some other options. The Lake Chapala Society sponsors day tours to various popular shopping locations like Guadalajara's Galerias Mall, Tonalá, and Tlaquepaque for 350 pesos round trip for members and 450 pesos for non-members. There's also a 3-day bus tour to a big shopping mall in McAllen, Texas.

One of the most popular tour and travel agencies is Charter Club Tours in Ajijic (bit.ly/2eTEt9X). It has a great selection of day trips as well as beach trips, and trips to other popular Mexican destinations (including the US border) on first-class buses.

There are other travel agencies throughout the area, as well. And there are individual tour operators, too, that have very good reputations, but that are less advertised. The best place to ask about these is at the Lake Chapala Society information booth. Or, check the free monthly local magazine Ojo del Lago, available at many locations.

Driving Your Own Car

You'll find that, in general, driving at Lakeside is very similar to driving north of the border.

- Driving is on the right side of the street.
- Traffic lights are the same colors of green, amber, and red, and they mean the same things. And, handicapped parking is similarly marked.

- Signs are shaped and colored similarly. For example, stop signs are red and have eight sides. The lettering just says "*Alto*" instead of "Stop."
- Road stripes are yellow and white—the same as north of the border.
- Parking is not allowed along curbs that are painted yellow.
- You're not allowed to block driveways. Most people will have a sign saying "*No Estacionarse*" (No Parking) on their garage door. Other times, you'll just see a red circle with a capital E and a cross line through it. Sometimes it'll also say "*Se usar grua*" (a tow truck will be used). If you disobey, your car could be towed and impounded by the police at your expense.
- You must wear seat belts.
- The use of cell phones while driving is prohibited, unless you are using hands-free equipment.
- Most people turn right on a red light after stopping.
- Turn signals are used similarly, except that on highways, big trucks ahead of you might give you a left turn signal when it's OK for you to pass them.
- One difference: you must engage your blinkers (hazard lights) when driving in reverse.

Driving is a little trickier, though, for a number of reasons. Speed is measured in kilometers per hour, so be sure to look for that indication (usually in red numbers) on your dashboard's speedometer. And, many of the streets, especially in the older parts of the towns, are very narrow, and they are one-ways. If someone has not parked right up to the curb on the left side, your rear-view mirror on the right side is in danger of grazing a telephone pole.

Similarly, when huge water trucks or garbage trucks come lumbering toward you, there may be no other choice than to back up to the last intersection to allow them to pass. Trucks also sometimes double park for a little while, holding up traffic. The cobblestones and speed bumps (*topes*), fortunately, keep traffic from speeding too much, although they do generate a lot of complaints.

In some of the older parts of the towns, there are street dogs who usually know when not to enter a street—but not always. And, children tend to play in the streets more than they do north of the border, so it's important to stay very alert. It helps a great deal to have consulted a map beforehand, so you know which streets are one-ways and more likely to be narrow.

Keep a special look-out for bicycles. Traffic laws do not pertain to them as they do north of the border, so they can be reckless with impunity.

Most people prefer not to drive at night not only because of the narrow streets but because there's a greater chance that pets and livestock may wander into the streets when there's not much traffic. Animals are not always fenced in.

You need **registration plates** on the car in order to drive legally in Mexico, but they don't need to be Mexican plates. In the state of Jalisco, it's OK if your foreign plates have expired (caution: it's not OK in Puerta Vallarta). The status of your Mexican vehicle importation permit is what matters. That's the document that came with the vehicle permit sticker on the inside of your windshield that you received when crossing the border. Remember that the original **temporary vehicle importation permit** that you got is only good for up to 180 days unless you have upgraded your own immigration status to a residence visa in the mean time. Always keep a copy of the temporary vehicle immigration permit document. Or better yet, keep a certified copy of it in your glove compartment. Don't put the original there. A certified copy can be made at a *Notaria Pública* office (See the Index under *Notario Público*).

You also need a **driver's license**. It can be from another country, but it cannot have expired. See the Index for more information about how to get a Mexican driver's license, if you cannot renew your foreign one online or by mail.

Under Jalisco law, if your car has been in the state longer than 6 months, it must comply with the state traffic law, which includes requirements for vehicles, such as having a current **smog check sticker**. This has to be done yearly on or before the month that corresponds to the last digit of your license plate, as follows.

Ending Plate Digit

1 – January	6 – July
2 – February	7 – August
3 – March	8 – September
4 – April	9 – October
5 – May	0 – November

If you have foreign plates with no numbers, just get a new sticker in January of each year. Although the fine for not having a valid sticker is about $100 USD, that fine is completely waived if you get the sticker within 15 days. For that reason, most people don't bother getting the sticker.

Various car repair shops at Lakeside can perform the smog check. To make sure you don't over-pay for this, be aware that the law says that the maximum a shop can charge for gas vehicles is 4 times the minimum daily wage, which currently comes to a total of 3600 pesos, or up to 5 times the minimum daily wage for diesel vehicles, which is 400 pesos.

Most **gasoline** stations in Mexico are franchised by the government. They have green signs saying "PEMEX," and they are well-run, clean, and efficient. The stations are full service only. That is, someone will come and pump the gas for you. If the attendant also washes the windshield, a tip of 5 pesos is customary.

Various gas stations do use a number of tricks to make more money. One is to not start the gas meter at zero if no one is looking. So, always check that the meter starts at zero. Another trick some stations use is to water down the gasoline, which probably also happens north of the border. On my online site LakeChapalaReporter.com, I do studies occasionally of which gas stations provide the best mileage for my car.

Gas stations sell two grades of gasoline: 87 octane, and 92 octane, plus diesel. Gasoline in Mexico costs about $4.00 USD per gallon (check bit.ly/2eP6pfl for current prices per liter). Gas stations take credit cards as well as cash. The one in Ajijic on the *carretera* (between Madero and Juan Alvarez streets) is open every day from 6am to 10pm or so.

Car Accidents

There's a saying that the first thing you should do if you're involved in a car accident in Mexico if it's your fault is to drive away. But, of course, I don't recommend that. Your insurance company won't pay the claim when you get caught (and you probably will, with a foreign plated car), they'll drop your policy, and you'll be in trouble with the police.

If there are any injuries, call **Cruz Roja** (Red Cross) for an ambulance. They're headquartered in Chapala. Their phone numbers are: **065** or 376-765-2308 (preferable). They used to be the only ambulance company allowed by law to serve accident victims, but that is no longer the case. So, if a different ambulance arrives, you can use it, too.

If the accident is minor, try to work out a financial agreement with the other driver. That means there won't be a police report, which means the insurance companies won't pay. But, the cost to fix the damages may be less than your deductible.

If you plan to call the police and/or your insurance agent, don't move either car, even if the cars obstruct traffic. If the police get involved, call your insurance company immediately, and get an agent to the scene of the accident quickly. Until the agent arrives and takes financial responsibility (which is what you have them for), the police considers you uninsured, even if you have your insurance policy with you. If the accident involves an injury, or if there's major damage to the vehicles or to other property, the police can place you under arrest and impound your car if they determine it was your fault.

> *"Until the agent arrives and takes financial responsibility (which is what you have them for), the police considers you uninsured even if you have your insurance policy with you."*

That's because vehicle accidents are considered criminal events. And that's why you need to make sure your car insurance never lapses, and that it covers bail bonds and legal expenses. Everything hinges on the insurance agent showing up to take over. And if you get arrested or they threaten to impound your car, call your lawyer, too. Both your insurance agent's and your lawyer's cell phone numbers should be in your cell phone, and on the Vehicle Accident Form located in the Appendix. You'll want to make sure you have a copy of it in your car.

> *"If the police determine that you were under the influence of alcohol or drugs, the insurance company will probably not represent you or pay for the claim. They'll probably also cancel your policy."*

If the police determine that you were under the influence of alcohol or drugs, the insurance company may not represent you or pay for the claim. They'll probably also cancel your policy.

If you find yourself in a legal bind, you can call the following lawyer.

Lic. Spencer McMullen
(045) 331-556-0828
Attorney and official court translator

Car Repairs

There are many places to get your car repaired Lakeside, from individual mechanics to larger repair facilities. Most of them are in the Riberas del Pilar *colonia* in Chapala, and in Jocotepec (lower rent areas). Most of them are very good, taking pride in being able to fix most problems. You will find that the labor cost is much lower than north of the border. Most places love to work on Chevys, Fords, Toyotas, and Nissans (which are made in Mexico) because the parts are widely available, and because fixing them is easier.

The smaller shops tend to specialize in such areas as automatic transmissions, mufflers and tailpipes, or suspension and wheel work. Sometimes they're the best at that specialty, but sometimes they're not. The wisest course is to find a good general-purpose shop or individual that has had experience with your type of car, and whom you trust. If they can't fix it, they'll know who can. They have their own network of trusted specialists—sometimes in Guadalajara.

How to find such a general-purpose shop? It's not necessarily the biggest shop on the *carretera*. It's often the individual genius mechanic working under his carport. Word of mouth recommendations are best. And at Lakeside for a newcomer, that means using online web boards and searching for keywords, such as "repair." See the Appendix for local web boards.

Car Insurance
Not all Mexican car insurance carriers will cover non-Mexicans or non-Mexican-plated vehicles. Your best option, at least at first, is to visit a brokerage that is popular

with other expats, and that can write coverage through at least several insurance companies. You'll have a better chance of getting the right policy for your vehicle and your needs. Vehicle insurance is less expensive in Mexico than north of the border.

By the way, many people who have an all-terrain vehicle, golf cart, scooter, or motorcycle, don't think they need insurance—or even registration for the vehicle—thinking that their chances of getting stopped is lower, and thinking they can self-insure for any damage their vehicle is capable of causing. Or, they license the vehicle just once to get the plates, and then neglect to follow up with renewals or insurance. I've seen quite a few golf carts scooting around the narrow streets of Ajijic without license plates. But if a child were to get knocked over by one coming around a corner, and she hit her head on the cobblestones, the medical expenses could be catastrophic, and the driver could easily end up in the pokey. Insurance premiums for these types of vehicles are often just as much as they are for regular cars (possibly because they're easier to steal). That's why people are willing to take the chance. But, even though the risk may be lower, the consequences are still high.

Most expats I have talked to use the following agency for their vehicle insurance. They're a good bet to at least start with. They're located on the *carretera* (it's called *Hidalgo* there) in the Riberas del Pilar *colonia* on the mountain side of the street between San Juan and San Lucas streets in a pumpkin-colored building.

Parker Insurance Services
Hidalgo #267
Riberas del Pilar
Chapala
Phone: 376-765-5287

The Parker agency also offers health, home, and travel insurance policies. You will be able to find other agencies, too, if you search for "insurance" on local web boards.

Buying or Selling a Vehicle

As explained earlier (Part 2 - Before Your Move, Chapter 6 - What About Your Car?), you can buy and sell a foreign-plated car privately from and to a non-Mexican using the loophole of buying a new temporary vehicle importation (TIP) license online.

You could also "nationalize" your car and get Jalisco license plates, making it easier to use as a trade-in. "Nationalizing" means officially importing the car. But, only certain cars qualify for nationalization. If your car qualifies, you can do it yourself by driving to the border to meet an auto customs agent.

Or, you can have someone else nationalize your car by driving it to the border for you. There have been many nationalization scams, though, so I don't recommend doing this without a lawyer involved.

Aside from the high cost of nationalizing your vehicle (probably between $2,500 and $3,000 USD), and the hassle involved, another downside of nationalizing your vehicle is that your insurance premiums will increase, and your coverage will be reduced. So, why would you want to nationalize your car? It's because you cannot own a foreign-plated car if you're a Mexican citizen or have a Residente Permanente visa (unless your spouse or partner is neither of those).

In short, the simplest way to get rid of your foreign-plated car is to use the new-TIP loophole (if you can find a local non-Mexican buyer who agrees to do this). The second-best option, especially if the car does not qualify for nationalization, is to drive it across the border and sell it there.

There are two car dealerships at Lakeside. First, there's a fairly new, small Chevrolet dealer for new cars only in the Centro Laguna Mall:

Chevrolet Centuria
333-770-2400

Then there's a larger one that sells many makes.

S & S Auto
Hidalgo #101 (the *carretera*)
Riberas del Pilar

They sell both new and used cars, and are considered reputable.

You may be able to find used cars for less money elsewhere, though (I noticed a used car/consignment car lot just next to them, recently). There are individual auto brokers to whom you can give your vehicle requirements, and they find it at a price you want to pay—for a fee. They cast their net farther than just Lakeside. I have seen good feedback on at least one such broker in the Lakeside area on the local web boards (see the Appendix).

To buy a car, the State of Jalisco requires you to have a CURP number and an RFC number (see Index) in order to prevent tourists from buying cars. Other Mexican states may not have this requirement.

You'll also see groups of cars along the *carretera* that have red fluorescent triangles on their roofs. Those are also for sale—usually by someone waiting there.
And, you can certainly inquire about cars anywhere that have For Sale or *Se Vende* written on them. You'll want to limit your choices to vehicles that have Jalisco plates, though, since plates from other states are more difficult to trace.

I highly recommend that you visit a knowledgeable lawyer when buying a used car or motorcycle. It's possible that there is money owed on it, or that it's stolen. If it's stolen, it

> *"To find out if a car is stolen, check website: bit.ly/2xv9DjF."*

will be confiscated when you apply for Jalisco license plates in your name. To find out if a car or motorcycle has been stolen, check this website: bit.ly/2xv9DjF.

Again, a lawyer I recommend in this area is:

Spencer McMullen
Hidalgo #230 (the *carretera*)
Chapala
Phone: 376-765-7553

Getting Your Car Out of Impound

If your car has been impounded for any reason, the police must give you the name and address of the impound yard where it's located.

Here are the requirements to have a *foreign-plated* car released.

- You need to pay the ticket, and to bring the paid receipt.
- If you're not the vehicle's owner, you need to bring a notarized power-of-attorney document showing that you're authorized to claim the vehicle on behalf of the owner.
- You need to bring the vehicle's title or a receipt from the country of origin.
- You need to bring your passport.

- You need to show that you are in the country legally by bringing your FMM tourist document or your residence visa card.
- You need to show that your vehicle is in the country legally by bringing your vehicle's temporary importation permit (TIP) document. This is the one you received when you crossed border. It should correspond to the window sticker. Or, bring the extended vehicle temporary importation permit you may have applied for when you received your residence visa.
- Present the original and one copy of all documents.

The requirements to have a *Mexican-plated* car released from impound are the same as for a foreign-plated vehicle, except that you need to bring your car's registration document instead of the vehicle temporary importation permit document, and the vehicle's *factura* (Mexican title/invoice).

Chapter 5

Shopping

Lakeside has an interesting mix of store types. That's because the communities here go back for centuries, long before supermarkets and "big box" stores became popular north of the border. Most areas here are not zoned in the way they are north of the border, and many locals here don't have cars, so the little mom-and-pop corner stores and the small specialty stores are what they're used to.

Guadalajara to the north, however, is modernizing fast, with Costcos, Sam's Clubs, Best Buys, Home Depots, Office Depots, and big modern shopping malls being developed in the city and in the suburbs. And, the Lakeside area is more and more becoming a suburb of Guadalajara. So, it's possible that someday, the Lakeside area will become a boutique area with big box stores on the outskirts, complete with McDonald's restaurants.

Those days aren't here yet, so we still have time to enjoy and support the traditional way of buying and selling goods. I, for one, am glad to be here while this way of life still exists. I like to see little old ladies walking around with their bags, carefully picking out the vegetables for the day's main meal like my grandmother did in Europe. I like the impromptu side-of-the-road barbeques. And I like to see the hand-woven rugs and serapes for sale hanging on tree limbs.

Mercados

There's a tradition in Mexico that every town has a central church, a plaza, and a *mercado*—all in close proximity. Those three features combined are considered the heart of a town. This tradition was established long before there were cars, of course, and it enabled people not to have to walk very far for their daily needs. A *mercado* is a street market, or common market, consisting of a group of booths (usually covered) that sells all the basics for every-day living, like food, clothes, and small toys and trinkets. It's usually open every day. The biggest one today is near the Chapala pier. But, not every town follows this pattern. For instance, San Antonio does not currently have a *mercado*, and neither does Ajijic, although they may have existed there at one time.

Supermercados

"Supermercado" translates to "supermarket," and is the name given to the big box stores like Walmart. It's also used by *mercados* with aspirations.

Tiendas

Tiendas are individual stores with signs on them, like grocery (*abarrotes*) stores. They have the daily basics of food and household supplies for a neighborhood. There are also specialty *tiendas* like stationery stores (*papelarías*), hardware stores (*ferreterías*), and laundries (*lavanderías*).

Tianguis (pronounced tee-ahng'-gees)
These are weekly outdoor flea markets where local farmers and craftsmen and women come to sell their wares. They're very popular with expats, providing opportunities to run into each other and chat. There you'll find produce, meats and fish, clothes, shoes, jewelry, all kinds of art (ceramic, beads, carved, paintings, and sculptures), bakery items, flowers, toys, pirated DVDs and CDs, and household utensils. At times, it's a little like a street fair, with roving marimba players, blaring mariachi music from speakers, street dogs, and beggars—all jostling together on cobblestones.

The most widely attended *tianguis* by expats is held on Wednesdays on Revolución street in Ajijic, just south of the *carretera*. It's geared toward expats in that the prices are a little higher and the produce is the very best. The weekly Chapala *tianguis* is just as large, but the wares and prices are geared more toward local Mexicans. The produce is more varied as to ripeness and perfection, and the prices are a little lower. You'll notice that the Chapala *tianguis* is more likely to have listed prices. There are other *tianguis*, as well. Some are in other towns, and some are just for niche items, like organically grown produce. The best way to find out about these (their locations sometimes change) is through the Lakeside web boards (see the Appendix).

The *tianguis* merchants only accept cash, so this is where your diligent study of Spanish numbers and money will pay off. You'll want to know how much something costs first, by asking, "Cuánto?" If it's something to eat, you'll also want to know what

> *"The tianguis merchants only accept cash, so this is where your diligent study of Spanish numbers and money will pay off. "*

the unit of measure is. Usually it's per kilo, which is around 2 pounds. Do some quick math in your head. If you're from the US, divide by 20 for a rough estimate For instance, if something costs *ciento cuarenta* pesos (140 pesos), dividing by 20 gives you $7 dollars. In this case, at 140 pesos equals about $7.92 USD. If you don't understand what a vendor is quoting you, pull out some paper and a pen, or your smartphone, and ask them to write down the number of pesos. They do this all the time.

If you're watching your budget carefully, you may want to write down in a notebook what you paid per kilo at that particular stall, and then comparison shop with the other stalls. Each stall usually stays in the same place from week to week. I've found that the Ajijic *tianguis*'s prices are comparable to Walmart's, but the quality of the produce is better at the *tianguis*. So, aside from wanting to patronize the smaller farms rather than Walmart, I buy most of my produce there—or at the Chapala *tianguis*.

You'll find that meat, poultry, fish, and seafood are not necessarily kept on ice. For that reason, you'll want to shop earlier in the day, rather than later, if you need those.

The only negative part of shopping at a *tianguis* is that the bags get heavy without having a shopping cart. This is where those giant, blue, IKEA bags that you brought down from north of the border (you did bring them, didn't you?) will come in handy. Take two of them to the *tianguis* so you can hang one from each shoulder. Then you can balance your load as you go. And, do watch your purse and bags carefully. It's a good place for pickpockets since people are close together and bump into each other, and are preoccupied.

If you want to negotiate prices at the *tianguis*, it's fair game for anything other than food staples. That doesn't mean that every merchant is willing to play the game. Some of their prices are firm—especially if other people are listening. Do offer a fair price, though, one that the merchant could say yes to. If you go too low, they'll just be offended, and you'll both lose face.

Buying Water

You most likely already know not to drink water directly from a faucet in Mexico unless the house has a purification system installed. But there is actually one neighborhood at Lakeside, Chula Vista, where it is said that the water is clean enough to drink since it has its own well system. And many people do that. But if you don't have a water purification system and don't live in Chula Vista, you'll only want to drink purified bottled water, including the water you make ice cubes with. By the way, you never have to worry about the water or ice cubes in restaurants Lakeside. They only use purified bottled water or have water purification systems. The street vendors might be a little more risky, though.

You can buy bottled water from a store or from water trucks that cruise through your neighborhood. The advantage of buying water from the trucks is that they will haul in the big 20-liter plastic *garrafóns* to your kitchen for you. They'll even put one in your dispenser for you. The *garrafóns* are the size of the ones used north of the border for water coolers, so they're heavy. And the older you get, the heavier they get.

> *"You never have to worry about the water or ice cubes in restaurants Lakeside. They only use purified bottled water or have water purification systems."*

You'll probably want to limit your choices of *garrafón* water brands to three of them: Ciel (which is purified by Coca-Cola), Santorini (Pepsi), and Bonafont (Group Danone, makers of Evian water and Activia yogurt). Those are the most trusted brands, using the best means of purification (reverse osmosis), and they are the only ones the *supermercados* like Walmart and Soriana carry. And they'll only take back empties for those three brands.

By the way, when you buy a *garrafón* of water, you're paying for the water and a deposit for the bottle itself. If you buy brands other than those top three from a water truck, that's the only place you can turn the empty *garrafóns* back in for a deposit return or exchange. So, if you buy an off-brand, you can only turn it back in or exchange it when that truck comes around again, which means you have to be home at that time, and hope that you recognize the particular tune it plays (like an ice-cream truck). And, I've heard unsubstantiated rumors that the off-brands may not have 100% purified water. For all those reasons, I recommend sticking with the top three brands. If you find yourself stuck with an off-brand empty *garrafón*, you can always place it outside with your garbage. Someone will undoubtedly take it off your hands and get a few pesos for it at a recycling center.

If you do use the big *garrafóns* of water, you'll need some kind of dispenser. Some people like the kind used north of the border, whereby you turn the *garrafón* upside-down into a plastic or metal or ceramic dispenser with a valve at the bottom. They require muscles, skills, and probably luck. But if you're game, you can buy them at some local *supermercados*, like Walmart and Soriana, or at Costco and Sam's Club (see the "Where to Buy Things" section below for more about these stores). You can buy ceramic ones at ceramic stores, who usually display them outside on the sidewalk or parking lot.

What I use is a metal holder, about waist high, with which I can easily tip the *garrafón* to dispense water. It does still require muscles to carry the *garrafóns* in and out of a shopping cart, in and out of the car, into the house and into the holder. But I can manage for a few more years.

Of course, you can always buy smaller plastic bottles of water at any store. They're easier to maneuver, use, and refrigerate, and there are no deposits. You can buy dispensers for these, too, if you want. I've seen people place a small water dispenser on their bathroom sinks, for instance, to use when brushing their teeth. A pitcher and glass work just as well, of course.

Buying Groceries

It's most convenient to shop at a *supermercado* like Walmart if you need to buy a wide range of items. The local Walmart is at the very east end of Ajijic, just across from where the *carretera* meets the Libramiento. It's similar to Walmarts north of the border, except for having a smaller selection of items in each category. But it does have categories that Walmarts north of the border don't carry, like motorcycles and mattresses.

Another *supermercado* in the area is Soriana. It's located just north of central Chapala on the Madero highway going north to Guadalajara. It's on the east side of the street between Avenida Pepe Guizar and Los Maestros streets.

Start looking for the tall red Soriana sign on your right as you go north after the PEMEX station on Madero. It's very much like Walmart, but it has more Mexican items. Those two stores know they're competing against each other, so they usually have price comparison signs along their aisles.

When you drive into shopping parking lots, you will probably be greeted by Mexican men with buckets and towels. They want to wash your car for you for a few pesos while you're shopping. They're very polite, so you can easily turn them down if you're not interested.

The quality of the produce in both stores can vary widely depending on the shipment received most recently. Remember that produce is usually sold by the kilogram, which is a little over 2 pounds.

Produce should be sanitized when you get home. This includes everything that has been grown with water, including unbagged nuts (but not spices). You don't need to purify produce that is either going to be peeled (oranges, avocadoes, bananas) or cooked (potatoes, onions). You could just make it a habit to purify all fruits and vegetables and nuts, though. It's very simple. I bought a plastic tub (about the size you might wash dishes in), and I put the produce in there, cover it with purified water, and add some drops of disinfectant (soaking in purified water alone won't kill any bacteria). I set my kitchen timer for 20 minutes, take the items out to drain on a towel or paper towels, and then put them away.

The most widely used disinfectants are MicroDyn and BacDyn, both of which can be found in the produce sections of the *supermercados*, and both contain the active ingredient ionized silver. Walmart also has its own "Great Values" branded one. These do not affect the taste of the fruits or vegetables or nuts. In a pinch, you can also use a small amount of chlorine bleach as a disinfectant, but that tends to leave a bleachy taste.

Having said all this, I got lazy a few years ago and stopped sanitizing produce I got from Walmart, and I've had no problems whatsoever. I also no longer sanitize raspberries and blueberries. I think it's because the berries come from the Driscoll farms located right across the lake, whose water quality is probably good. It's the produce that comes from the big Guadalajara markets (like at the *tianguis*, and at some of the smaller *tiendas*) that are the most problematic because they are sometimes shipped in from southern areas of Mexico that have lower irrigation water quality. So, either sanitize or not at your own risk.

> *"Produce should be sanitized when you get home."*

In the bakery departments, you don't bag your own items as you would north of the border. You take a big, circular, metal tray (like a pizza pan) and tongs from the bakery counter, and then place each item you want on the tray. Then you take the tray back to the bakery counter, and the person there bags it for you, and places price stickers on the bags. That is, unless the items, like cakes, are already packaged and have a price sticker.

In general, you'll see differences in product packaging. There are more bags and fewer boxes, probably for the sake of cost and space. Powdered detergent and cat litter frequently come in bags, for instance, unless you buy a north of the border brand, in which case the price is much higher. Almost everything is priced more for a Mexican grocery budget, which is anywhere from a third to a half of what a grocery budget would be north of the border.

One of the big surprises is that eggs are not refrigerated in stores here. And they seem to be fine that way. I refrigerate them right away when I get home, and I have never found any spoiled eggs. You'll find that the Mexican butter is a deeper yellow, and has a deeper flavor, too. For myself, I prefer the more subtle flavor of imported butter, even though it costs more. In either case, you have to look carefully to see whether the butter has salt (*con sal* – with salt) or not (*sin sal* – without salt). The saltless butter is more plentiful in the dairy cases.

There are two other, smaller *supermercados* that expats are drawn to because they carry more north-of-the-border items and brands. One is El Torito, located in Plaza Bugambilias (the Mexican translation of the beautiful bougainvilleas flowering vine), which is on the south side of the *carretera* in Ajijic between Revolución and Juan Alvarez streets. Another is Super Lake, located on the south side of the *carretera* in San Antonio between Independencía and San José streets. The prices in these stores seem to be higher than in Walmart and Soriana because most of their products are imported. But if you simply must have B&M baked beans, they're the only places that have them.

Most of the *supermercados* are open from early morning into the evening every day, as opposed to smaller *mercados* and *tiendas,* which are more likely to only have one shift of workers. Smaller *tiendas* usually close at 2pm on Saturdays, and are closed on Sundays. But, even the large supermercados don't have 3rd shift night workers, the way they do north of the border. You will see big floor-washing machines in operation among the aisles during the day, people sweeping, and items being shelved from pallets all day long.

> *"Smaller tiendas usually close at 2pm on Saturdays, and are closed on Sundays."*

The check-out lanes are very similar to the ones north of the border. They're almost all computerized, and all the bigger stores take credit and debit cards. In fact, Soriana and Walmart will give you cash back from your credit or debit card.

It's still a cash society here in many ways, though. That's why it's important to know your Mexican numbers and money. The checkout people are mostly honest, but there are a few who know that expats don't always count their change correctly, and take advantage of it by shortchanging them a few pesos here and there. Also, sometimes bar code prices are wrong, so do watch the monitors as items are being scanned. It sometimes also happens that the prices listed on the shelves are wrong. You can certainly question any discrepancies you find. But business is not as efficient here as it is north of the border. There are more unintentional errors, many seemingly routine transactions take more time, and sometimes you'll have to make a few trips back and forth that would not be necessary north of the border. Time and efficiency are not as important in this slower-paced society.

"Give a tip to people who bag your groceries. They're not store employees."

Before you leave a store, give a tip to the people who bag your groceries. They're not store employees. They "volunteer," and hope for nice tips. Some have families to support, and it's their only job. Five to ten pesos is fine.

When you wheel your cart out to your car, you'll often find the same car wash guys now offering to help you load your groceries into your car, for a small fee. Again, feel free to accept or decline, as you wish.

Wherever you go to shop, or even just walking around in neighborhoods, you're bound to meet with people begging. Some are blind, some are disabled in some other way, and some ask for contributions to various charities. It's up to you how to respond, of course, but it's best to think about how you'd like to respond in advance. For myself, I prefer to contribute to charities directly, rather than through individuals who might be tempted to dip into their cash box to buy lunch every day. The *Cruz Roja* (Red Cross), for instance, can be contributed to through PayPal. Just ask the *Cruz Roja* table at the Lake Chapala Society how to do that.

For individuals, you could establish a policy that you'll only give away 30 pesos per day to the disabled, for instance. That way, you'll feel that you're contributing, but that you're setting boundaries, too. And some people decline in general to give people money on the street. The reasoning is that it contributes to demeaning the beggar and to a cycle of dependency. Thanks, in part, to the influx of expats, there are now many local charities with funds to help almost everyone who needs it, and to help them learn new skills—especially children. Another way to contribute, of course, is to volunteer your services at those charities.

Speaking of children, you will see some selling berries during what should be school hours for them. They have been hired out by their parents to brokers, instead of going to school. The brokers set sales quotas for the children, and if they don't meet them, they get punished by the brokers and by their parents. For that reason, many of them are quite aggressive in their pursuit of gringos, in particular. This form of child exploitation is against the law in Jalisco, but it is not always enforced. My own policy is not to purchase anything from children.

Where To Buy Things

You can find everything you need Lakeside, if you know where to look. You may not be able to find everything you *want* at Lakeside, but I can tell you a few places to look for those things, too.

As I mentioned earlier, the first things you're going to need when you arrive are spare keys, especially if you can be locked out while in an enclosed back or side yard. I recommend a particular locksmith and key store because they do a good job of filing down the metal burs, which can make the difference between the keys working smoothly or not—or not working at all, so you have to go back again to have them re-filed. It's a small, yellow shack on the corner of Revolución and the *carretera* (the main highway) in Ajijic. It's called *Cerrajería Cardenas* (Locksmith Cardenas), and it's located on Revolución street (the one where the Ajijic *tianguis* is on Wednesdays) to the east side of the Bugambilias Plaza, right next to Salvador's Restaurant.

Most houses Lakeside are rented or sold as furnished, knowing that it usually isn't cost-effective for expats to bring their own furniture with them. So, you may not need furniture right away. But if you do, or if you'd like to pick up some decorations or art pieces, your best values come from resale shops and thrift stores, sometimes called bazaars (or bazars). You'll find many of them all along the *carretera*, and in central Ajijic. Some of these shops carry both used and new items, so they're always fun to browse, whether or not you're looking for anything in particular.

You can also have fun looking at yard sales, which are usually called bazaars (or bazars), too. There are also advertisements listed on bulletin boards at the Lake Chapala Society and at popular expat stores like El Torito, Super Lake, Walmart, and Soriana for items for sale or items wanted. Local periodicals, like the monthly El Ojo de Lago magazine, also have classified advertising in the back. New furniture, appliances, ceramics, house decorations, linens, and clothes can also be found at Lakeside just by exploring. But you may find the selection somewhat limited based on what you're used to.

The next places to look are in Guadalajara. There are four places I recommend for you to explore next.

1. The first is the *López Mateos* group of "big box" stores. This is the only place beyond Lakeside that I recommend newcomers can drive to alone for shopping. What's there is a big Walmart store, a Mega store (like Walmart), a Costco, a Sam's Club, an Office Depot, and a Home Depot. The Costco and Sam's Club are membership stores, so you'll want to bring your membership card from north of

the border with you, or bring your passport as identification if you want to become a member. It costs something like $40 dollars. The way to get there is to take the Lakeside *carretera* west, and then look for the sign as you approach Jocotepec to take the right turnoff to Guadalajara. This is a road that merges onto Highway 54 (Guadalajara-Morelia) going north to Guadalajara. It's also called the Guadalajara-Colima Highway, and as you go north on it, it's also called the Guadalajara-López Mateos Sur (which means South). After about 30 minutes of going north, right after the town and golf course of Santa Anita, you'll see the big stores on the right. The Office Depot and the Home Depot are a mile or so farther up on that same highway.

2. The next place I recommend is the Galerias Mall. The two anchor department stores in the mall are Sears and Liverpool. The Sears store is more upscale than the Sears stores are north of the border. You'll hardly recognize it. The quality is more like Macy's. And, the Liverpool store is very upscale and expensive—more like Saks Fifth Avenue. And then there are some interesting smaller stores in the mall. If you're really hungry for McDonald's or Dairy Queen or Krispy Kreme's, they're there, too. Plus, this mall is surrounded by a Walmart, a Mega store, a Costco, and a Best Buy. Most of these places will deliver big items Lakeside for you. The way to get there, at

Living at Lake Chapala: Shopping

least for the first time, is by taking a tour bus. You can buy your round-trip ticket for about 450 pesos at the Lake Chapala Society. The trip is an hour drive in complete luxury each way, and your purchases can be stored underneath the bus in the big cargo areas.

3. My next recommendation is the town of Tonalá on the east end of Guadalajara. It's a major trading center for Mexican handcrafted gifts and decorative items, such as furniture, blown glass, papier maché, ceramics and more. The prices run from inexpensive to expensive, and everything in between. In fact, many of the handcrafted items you see in stores Lakeside are wholesaled from Tonalá. Visiting Tonalá is part of a 1-day tour offered by the Lake Chapala Society and by Charter Tours and Travel in Ajijic. Both tours combine shopping in the town of Tonalá with shopping in the town of Tlaquepaque on the same day since the towns are close together.

4. The town of Tlaquepaque is also a trading center of handcrafted items. These tend to be more upscale and gallery-worthy items, like one-of-a-kind art pieces, jewelry, artisan furniture and decorative items. It's well worth visiting, even if the items may be a little out of your price range. As with most handcrafted items in Mexico, you can try negotiating a price that suits your budget.

If you're interested in plants for home and garden, you'll find you're in paradise. Lakeside is lush with plants all year around, and there are many nurseries (*viveros*) here. One of the largest is Flora Exotica, which is located on the northwest corner of the Libramiento and the *carretera*. There's another nice one beside Telecable on the south side of the *carretera* in the Riberas del Pilar neighborhood between San Juan and San Jorge streets. You'll see *viveros* signs all along the *carretera*, in fact. And if you particularly like cacti, many of the *viveros* west of Ajijic specialize in them. Seeds are a little more difficult to come by. The garden center two doors east of 7-Eleven on the corner of the *carretera* and San Mateo in Riberas Del Pilar has a few flower, vegetable, and herb seeds, and so do some hardware stores. But many people also buy them online north of the border, and have them sent. You can check local web boards (see the Appendix) for peoples' online recommendations.

For those who are used to having an Office Depot nearby north of the border, there are none Lakeside. As mentioned above, there is one on Highway 54 in Guadalajara that's not hard to get to (although it will take about an hour to drive there). You can also Google "Office Depot Guadalajara" or "Office Max Guadalajara" for other locations if you feel adventurous. The reason this is significant is that the *supermercados* Lakeside have very few paper and office supplies. What they have are school supplies, basically. There are many stationery stores (*papelarías*) everywhere, but they're not quite what you'd expect—concentrating, again, on school supplies. They do have copiers, fax machines, and sometimes public computers, though. But it would appear that very few locals have need of legal pads, full-size staplers, and the like.

By the way, if you're looking for pads of paper online at Office Depot or Office Max, they're not in the "paper" section (as Google translates it), they're in the subsection called "blocks" (which means paper pads) within the "Office" section.

The closest Craigslist for this area is the Guadalajara one. But there don't seem to be many listings for merchandise there, for some reason. However, many online stores, like eBay and Amazon, do allow purchases from Mexico for a higher shipping fee, and an approximately 10 day shipping time for regular government mail service. This is where having a mailing service comes in handy, since vendors don't have to ship internationally. There is another online store you can look at, too. It's a Mexican version of eBay (without an auction) called <u>Mercado Libre</u>, and you can get new and used merchandise shipped to your home from there. You'll want to make sure you're in the Mexican version of Mercado Libre since there are number of them for various Latin American countries.

What You Won't Find

Because most people north of the border work away from their homes, industries there have developed products to support that lifestyle. A prime example is **frozen meals**, like Lean Cuisine™. In contrast, most Mexicans who live in small towns have at least one adult, usually the woman of the house, who does not work outside the home. They're expected to cook. So the need for frozen meals is not as strong as it is north of the border. Also, frozen food requires stores to spend more on electricity for freezers, and electricity is comparatively expensive in Mexico. The result? No Lean Cuisine™ yet. Some frozen food is starting to appear here, though. There are pizzas, shaped hamburgers, French fries, a little Chinese food, and a few appetizers like flautas in the frozen food sections. And there are lots of bagged cut vegetables as there are north of the border. But not full meals, to speak of. Fortunately for us expats, the *supermercados* do have rotisserie chickens for quick meals. And, Costco and Sam's Club do have some frozen lasagnas and Chinese food that are very good. A cottage industry is also developing by expats at the local markets to fill this need. Expats are making and selling frozen meals themselves, like meatloaf, quiches, chili, and other north-of-the-border comfort foods.

"No Lean Cuisine™ yet."

But speed is not what meals are all about here. Meals are still a time for everyone in the family to be together. The main meal of the day is called the *comida*, and it usually lasts from 2pm to 4pm, with multiple courses. Then, families will have a smaller meal in the late evening, around 9pm called the *cena*. So, **fast food restaurants** haven't arrived here yet, either. You have to go into Guadalajara to find a McDonald's or a Burger King. Dominos Pizza does have a small restaurant and delivery store here in the little plaza to the west of Walmart on the *carretera*. I stopped in there for lunch one day, hoping for a slice, but they only make whole pizzas, and it would have taken 15 minutes to make. When I did order a full pizza, I found the sauce spicier than north of the border.

There's one other item that eluded me for a while: **bug repellent containing the chemical DEET**. What I found out was that the acronym DEET is often not used here. The entire chemical name is spelled out in the ingredients list, which is: dietil-meta-toluomida. "OFF Family" in an orange aerosol can has it in 15% strength. That can be found at Walmart, as well as in all pharmacies. There are two other brands containing DEET: Ultrathon and H24. They have stronger doses of DEET, but are a little harder to find. Incidentally, the stronger doses of DEET do not make the product more effective, it just lasts longer.

Incidentally, Mexico has a consumer protection agency called PROFECO, if you want to file a complaint about any product or vendor. You can do that on the website at: bit.ly/2wvy4Z1. You'll probably need a lawyer, though, to navigate the paperwork and to represent you. This is a very powerful organization, which has the authority to fine merchants more money than you're owed, making it easier for merchants to give in to your legitimate claims.

Chapter 6

Crime and Safety

Had this book been written in 2011, the subject of safety would not have merited its own chapter. But enough has changed to cause people both at Lakeside and north of the border to take a look at the issue of safety in determining whether the Lake Chapala area is a good place for expats to live.

In May of 2012, 18 Lakeside Mexicans were kidnapped, and their mutilated bodies were found a few weeks later a little north of Lakeside. These horrific acts were determined to be drug cartel-related, although it was reported that the victims had not been involved in the drug trade.

These were terrorist acts committed 1-1/2 months prior to the national presidential elections held on July 1st. Some political analysts have said these acts were committed in order to show that the ruling party was ineffective in the war against drugs, its central theme, and that the cartels are still in control of the country. Others have said that this scenario was inevitable as the major cartels try to claim one of the last remaining undominated areas of Mexico, and that the timing was coincidental.

Whatever the reasons, Lakeside residents, both locals and expats, were stunned. Daily life almost came to a standstill.

The local and state police arrived, as did the military. Many, possibly most, of the perpetrators were caught, and their safe houses and weapons caches were found. There were widespread rumors that many expats were going to leave, but no mass exodus actually occurred. To date, no other major incidents of this kind have been reported in this area, and the presence of the police and the military has subsided.

It's an unfortunate fact that there are destructive elements in every society, whether it's highly developed or not. Most of the time, these elements aren't noticed by average citizens, like the workings of the Mafia and other pervasive criminal organizations north of the border. They only become apparent when their fault lines rupture. But, after the shaking stops, life begins again, often with a deeper appreciation for life and the community. And that is what has happened here.

Overall, the crime problems at Lakeside are about what you'd expect in any community of this size. The expats generally have more money than the locals do, so it would be hard to imagine that there would not be the occasional house burglary and theft and vandalism. But these do not dominate conversations here.

> *"The chances that you'll be a victim of crime here are small."*

Statistically, unless you are involved in the drug trade, you are actually safer in Mexico than you are anywhere north of the border.

There is less fear here on a day-to-day basis than in any place I have lived north of the border. There are no roving gangs, and children play unsupervised in their neighborhoods—even into the evenings. I have never seen a woman of any age, local or expat, leered at or been made to feel uncomfortable in any way on the streets. Quite the opposite, in fact.

This is not to say that expats don't need to act prudently. Houses and cars should be locked, money should not be visible, and expensive jewelry should be kept to a minimum. And you should avoid walking alone at night—especially if you've been drinking. That's just common sense in any community.

In summary: the fear of crime should not be a reason for you to stay away from Lake Chapala. The chances that you'll be a victim of crime are small.

Chapter 7
Medical Care

The primary reason many people consider moving to Mexico is that the cost of living here is lower. A large part of that cost is for health care, for insurance, services, and medications. Aside from costs, quality of care is also a consideration, of course.

Medicare
Health care considerations require more thought at age 65 for US citizens, in particular, since that's the age when they become eligible for free health services through the government's Medicare program. To date, a Medicare benefit claim is only valid if the service is performed within the US or its territories—with two exceptions. The first exception is if you can prove you are just a tourist in Mexico, and that the service is the result of an emergency. The second exception is if the hospital from which you get the service (in Mexico or in Canada) is closer than the closest hospital in the US that can treat your medical condition. Until the day Medicare covers claims routinely from Mexico (if ever), US senior

"A Medicare benefit claim is only valid if the service is performed within the US or its territories—with two exceptions."

expats will need to decide whether their health needs can be met here. For most expats, the answer will be yes.

Quality of Medical Care

There are very good general practitioner doctors Lakeside, some of whom have graduated from and/or interned at very good US and Canadian medical schools and facilities. Most speak English, and take much more time with their patients than doctors do north of the border. You can count on at least a half hour with the doctor per visit. They're not pressured to go from one patient to the next in as short a time as possible.

There are also labs and clinics here that are well regarded. The Lakeside doctors and clinics may not have the fanciest equipment or high-rent facilities, but most of them are competent, caring, and knowledgeable enough to do a good job, and to know when to refer you to a specialist at Lakeside, or to one less than an hour away in Guadalajara, which has world-class medical specialists and hospitals. The Hospital Mexicano-Americano, for instance, has international health certification. And in Mexico City, the ABC Hospital (American British Cowdray Hospital) is also a world-class teaching and research facility, with board certified specialists.

As this edition is being published, there are two new hospitals being constructed Lakeside. One is on the south side of the Carretera across from Chula Vista Golf Course, and the other is on the west side of the Libramiento across from the El Dorado condos.

Incidentally, you don't need any referrals to go to a specialist. And, you can just walk into any clinic or lab, and ask for tests of any kind—blood work, urinalysis, whatever you think you need. And you'll get the results to take with you.

Cost of Medical Care
Most medical services and medications are from 40% to 70% lower than north of the border. For instance, going to a lab and having blood drawn to determine my blood type cost me about $10.00 USD at the Hospital Ajijic on the *carretera*. A visit to a doctor will cost between $35 and $100 USD, and most doctors will make house calls, if needed. Doctors frequented by gringos usually charge higher fees, but that doesn't necessarily mean better services.

Why is the cost of medical care here so much lower? Aside from lower wages, there are almost no medical malpractice suits here, so medical malpractice insurance premiums are lower, and there's no need to order redundant or unnecessary tests, either.

Pharmacies
The pharmacy chain most popular with gringos Lakeside seems to be Farmácia Guadalajara, which has a number of stores along the *carretera*. They're open 24/7, and they're among the few that will give you an official *factura*

(invoice/receipt) for your medications. The other one that will give you an official *factura* Lakeside is the Walmart pharmacy. The reason this is important is that an official *factura* is required by insurance companies for reimbursement of medications. If your medications are part of your treatment for an insurance-covered accident or illness, you'll want to go to either of those two pharmacies. If not, you can certainly go to any of the "*similares*" pharmacies you'll see at Lakeside. They sell discounted drugs, which are usually generics. These pharmacies keep their costs low by accepting only cash, which not only eliminates credit card fees, it allows them to under-report their sales figures to the government. And that's may be why they won't give you an official *factura*.

> "*An official factura is required by insurance companies for reimbursement of medications.*"

The generic drugs Lakeside are like generic drugs anywhere: they're great if they work for you, but in some cases, they may not have the same effect as branded drugs. But, I'm not aware of any poor quality issues for these generics, so they may be worth a try at a reduced cost.

Branded medications are actually already much less expensive than north of the border. My own medications from Farmácia Guadalajara are 75% less than what I would have to pay north of the border (without insurance), and they don't require prescriptions, so I save on doctor's visits, too.

Also, do ask the pharmacy you choose whether they give discounts for DIF or INAPAM discount card holders (see Index for more information on these). Some do, which can save you even more money.

> *"In Mexico, pharmacists do not need to have the extensive education and licensing required north of the border."*

And, lastly, be aware that in Mexico, pharmacists do not need to have the extensive education and licensing required north of the border. This means that you need to make sure that your doctor is aware of all the medications you're taking in order to prevent medication conflicts.

Dental Care

Mexico in general is known for being a dental care tourist destination. The quality and costs of care are so good that people plan their vacations in Mexico, in part, to get their teeth fixed or to be fitted for dentures. The Lake Chapala area is no exception. There is an abundance of excellent English-speaking dentists, many of whom can easily be found by cruising the *carretera*. Here is an article comparing popular dentists Lakeside: bit.ly/2x8c0Yc.

Choosing Your Medical Professionals

Your best choices are usually found by referral. The web boards (see the Appendix) frequently have comments about various doctors and dentists, so those are excellent places to begin your research. You could also ask your Mexican health insurance agent which doctor(s) the gringos go to.

There's also quite a bit of plastic surgery tourism Lakeside. Here's an article comparing popular plastic surgeons here: bit.ly/2h8csMH.

Cruz Roja (Red Cross)

The Cruz Roja in Mexico is a non-profit organization that assists victims of natural disasters and accidents. Cruz Roja ambulances used to be the only ones authorized to assist accident victims, but private ambulance companies are now also authorized. Cruz Roja has its own clinics, to which they drive accident victims for initial stabilization. What makes Cruz Roja services so special is that their services are free to those who cannot afford to pay, which makes them a critical community resource for low income locals and expats. For additional information, see their website at cruzrojachapala.com. Their phone number is in the Appendix.

> *"What makes Cruz Roja services so special is that their services are free to those who cannot afford to pay."*

Medical Clinics

There are a number of clinics at Lakeside that are open around the clock for emergencies. They also offer walk-in laboratory and x-ray services, or they have special arrangements with local providers of these services. Aside from the Cruz Roja clinic mentioned above, there is the Maskaras Clinic (which also has ambulance services) on the *carretera* (Hidalgo 79-G) in the Riberas Del Pilar *colonia* of Chapala. The nearest cross-street is San Jorge. Their website is here: maskarasclinic.com. Another clinic, which has actually recently been upgraded to a hospital is Hospital Ajijic, which also has an ambulance service, located on the *carretera* in Ajijic at #33. The cross street is Javier Mina. This one is used by many expats, and is run by physicians from Guadalajara. Both the Maskaras Clinic and the Hospital Ajijic have beds, but they do not have the extensive equipment and staff specialists that are found in the hospitals in Guadalajara. As mentioned previously, as this edition is going into print, two new hospitals are being built here (see the Quality of Medical Care section above).

IMSS Insurance

Although the cost of medical services is much lower in Mexico than north of the border, a serious illness or surgery can still be financially devastating. A heart attack could cost $10,000 USD, for instance, for full treatment and stabilization, and hospitals do want to be paid when the patient leaves, in addition to wanting $1,000 USD for admittance.

Some expats self-insure. That is, they have either enough money to pay for full treatment in Mexico, or they have enough money to pay for medical stabilization in Mexico, and then to pay for medical helicopter fare to the US to be covered by Medicare for full recovery. Other expats feel that they are at low risk for health problems, and save a certain amount of money every month toward medical bills rather than pay insurance premiums. For everyone else, some form of medical insurance is a good idea.

One of the basic insurance programs in Mexico comes from the Mexican Institute of Social Security, or IMSS. It has many services and facilities, including running its own outpatient clinics and general hospitals. It's very much like an HMO insurance organization in the US. IMSS also has pharmacy services, but there are many complaints that this is almost a useless benefit since they are poorly stocked, and rarely have the medication needed. And, they don't reimburse expenses from other non-IMSS pharmacies.

By law, all Mexican nationals have to be offered this insurance by their employers. And foreigners who have a residence visa (either a Residente Temporal or a Residente Permanente) visa are qualified to join. There's usually no medical exam, but not everyone is accepted. The application to join includes questions about pre-existing health conditions, which may cause some coverage to be excluded. And, coverage is phased in over a period of three years.

There is a waiting period of between 6 to 9 months, too. The annual premiums (in pesos) for 2017 are:

        Age   40-49 $4,750.00
        Age   50-59 $5,050.00
        Age   60-69 $7,300.00
        Age   70-79 $7,650.00
        Age   80 plus $7,700.00

Applications are only accepted in January and February, and in July and August. Here is the website for more information: imss.gob.mx.

Expats who join IMSS usually do so for the hospital benefits as a fall-back plan. The day clinics get very crowded, so you could easily end up waiting all day in a very noisy waiting room to get treatment. And the doctors and support staff don't always speak English. You'll want to bring a translator, although you may get lucky and find a bilingual patient in the waiting room. The doctors usually work there part-time, and then have their own practice, as well, so you never know whom you're going to get. But, it's better than nothing, and will certainly help in a dire health situation. It's best to contact a lawyer (*abogado*) or other facilitator who knows how the system operates with regard to expats. You can also research expats' experiences with IMSS on the local web boards (see the Appendix). Some say that because IMSS is required for all employees, expats get served last.

When researching whether certain procedures are covered, make sure you find out how much money will actually be paid. It's nice to be covered, but if the payment limit is low, it may not seem like such a good deal. Also, make sure you find out what coverage really means. For instance, does it include a room, food, the surgeon, anesthesiologist, nursing staff, and supplies? Sometimes these line items are not included in treatment quotes, and can make a big difference.

Seguro Popular Insurance

Another Mexican government health insurance program is called Seguro Popular. It's paid for by national sales taxes. Like IMSS, it includes clinics, hospitals, and pharmacies. You cannot be a member of Seguro Popular if you have any other insurance, though, including IMSS. In fact, it was established for Mexicans who could not afford IMSS, or were not qualified for it. Foreigners who have their residence visas do qualify, though.

The annual fees are calculated on a sliding scale based on income, but it's usually free for retirees. It's generally used by expats for the free and near-free medications and vaccinations. The down-side is that the outpatient clinics are just as crowded and noisy as the IMSS ones. Here is the main website: bit.ly/2xFpZ9f, And here is an article series regarding Seguro Popular: bit.ly/2whgwVv.

Private Health Insurance

There are many options in this category, but, generally, private health insurance in Mexico consists of what is referred to north of the border as "major medical." That is, it covers only hospitalizations and associated costs. It does not cover routine doctor visits or prescriptions. That's because those are considered inexpensive enough that most people can afford to pay for them out of their own pockets. Some expats have both the IMSS insurance and their own private insurance, and they pick and choose services and providers based on the individual medical situation.

> *"Some expats have both IMSS insurance and their own private insurance, and they pick and choose services and providers based on the individual medical situation."*

There are Mexican health insurance companies, and there are international health insurance companies. Many Mexican ones will not write a new policy to a person who is 65 years old or older, and they routinely cancel policies when a person turns 75 or so. Here is an article on private health insurance: bit.ly/2ww1OoK. What is most important is to make sure that the health insurance underwriting company is officially authorized by the federal government. If it isn't, it is not legally obligated to pay any claims. These non-authorized companies may sound great, may be based in the US, and may even pay most of their claims in order to build a good reputation in an area. But, if you get a serious illness, and the claims start getting expensive, they can just refuse to pay, and you have no legal recourse. It happens all the time, and it's heartbreaking. They seem to target baby boomers, too, unfortunately. Here is a website listing all the officially authorized health insurance underwriters in Mexico: bit.ly/2xERT59. Do not sign a health insurance policy that is not underwritten by one of those companies. Best Doctors is an example of a health insurance company that seems to be popular here. But it is not authorized in.

A good place to start is at an insurance broker's office. Many expats I've talked to use the following broker for their health insurance and their auto insurance.

Parker Insurance Services
Hidalgo #267
Riberas del Pilar
Chapala
Phone: 376-765-4070, or 376-765-5287

Private health insurance in Mexico is much less expensive than north of the border, but it is still a significant cost. Someone in their 60s without extensive medical problems can expect to pay between $5,000 and $10,000 USD per year, depending on deductibles. And, those figures rise a minimum of 15% every year. Again, that's for major medical coverage only.

Many people decide that it's not worth it, given all the other choices.

You'll also want to consider having coverage for emergency medical evacuation service to the US or Canada

> *"You'll also want to consider having coverage for emergency medical evacuation service to the US or Canada if you have family there, Medicare, a special clinic, or if you'd just feel more comfortable there."*

if you have family there, Medicare, a special clinic, or if you'd just feel more comfortable there. And, of course, you'll want to find out what is included and excluded, and whether the insurance payout is on a percentage basis of the charges, and if there's a maximum payment limit. Here is an article comparing these services: bit.ly/2fp1bYk.

Chapter 8
Home Life and Services

For most expats, everyday life in Lake Chapala revolves around people, animals, nature, and favorite pastimes like writing, reading, art, other hobbies, exploring, volunteering, and travel. At least, that seems to be the ideal. In order to have the time for these interests, your home life and services need to be reasonably stable. This is an area where you'll find many differences between what you're used to north of the border and here in Mexico. To be candid, Mexico is not known for its efficiency. You'll be surprised at all the conveniences you took for granted north of the border. It takes more time, more trips, and more patience to get your home services and technology up and running smoothly, and maintained, unless you live an extremely austere life here (which is not a bad idea, either).

Part of the challenge is the language barrier, but that's not the major part. If you can afford home services like a housekeeper and a gardener, there are schedules to maintain. Figuring out how to use your home phone and cell phone, and how to dial various places can be challenging, too. But, once these are learned and set up, your time will be freed up to enjoy the more satisfying aspects of your new life here in Lake Chapala.

Household Help

You will most likely be able to afford more household help at Lake Chapala than you could north of the border because wages are much lower here. The minimum wage in the US is $7.25 USD per **hour**, and the minimum wage in Mexico about $4.50 USD per **day**. That's the minimum wage employers must abide by, but not everyone does. There are certainly many rogue businesses that set their own rules, and only report to the government what they choose to report.

> *"Hiring household help is generally considered an informal cash arrangement, one that doesn't need to be reported to the government."*

Domestic employees are a special class of employees who only require minimal employer obligations. Hiring household help is generally considered an informal cash arrangement, one that does not need to be reported to the government. But it does have its own customs and expectations that you will want to abide by as a good member of the community.

1. You only need a verbal understanding to hire household help. However, a written agreement detailing work duties and schedules and amount paid per hour is a very good idea.
2. You're expected to pay only in cash, and on a weekly basis. If the person works several times per

week, the cash should be paid on the last expected work day of the week.
3. You are expected to pay 15 days worth of wages as a Christmas bonus (*aguinaldo*) on or before the 20th of December. This can be prorated if the person has not worked for you for a full year. To calculate how much is expected, figure out how much the person usually earns per day, and then multiply that times 15. As an example, suppose you've agreed to pay a person 200 pesos per week for services (regardless of how many days they come or hours they work). They're making 29 pesos per day (200 divided by 7). Multiply that times 15 days, and you owe them 435 pesos for *aguinaldo*. If they only worked half of the year for you, you only owe them half that, but it's Christmas, so it's easy to be more generous.
4. You're also expected to pay a minimum of 6 days wages, plus 25% of that, after each year the employee has worked for you.
5. You will, of course, want to give as much notice as possible if you intend to discontinue his or her services (without formal cause). You're expected to pay three month's wages severance pay, plus 20 extra days pay for each year he or she has worked for you.

Locals who work for gringos tend to ask for more money per hour than they would for a Mexican employer, and, if they come well recommended, they get it. The norm in this area seems to be between 50 and 70 pesos per hour for a housekeeper. It's more for gardeners and handymen because men here make more than women do.

If you rent your house, you may have inherited a gardener and/or a housekeeper as part of the lease. In that case, the issue of wages is not a concern for you, and neither is hiring or firing. But that isn't necessarily a good thing. In the case of a housekeeper, if you prefer not to be home when she's there (because you have to keep moving around to keep out of her way), that means that she will have keys to your house, and free access to everything in your home, which could be a security concern. Thefts can occur that way, especially if she lends the keys or copies them for someone else. Or, you have to arrange to be home whenever she's scheduled to be there. That ties you down to a schedule which you may or may not like. And, if one of her kids gets sick, she may not show up, and she may not call, but you still have to be there as if she were going to come. Your time will therefore no longer be your own, to a certain extent.

The same is true for gardeners who have to go through your house to get to the back or side yard. And if it turns out to be a housekeeper or gardener you're not fond of, you don't have the authority to make a change. You can, of course, complain to your landlord, but that could just make for more discomfort. So, do think about these issues before signing a lease.

If you want to hire your own domestic help, you will have more flexibility. First, only hire one that comes well recommended from someone you trust. Since you're a newcomer, it will probably be your rental agent, someone at the Lake Chapala Society, or a friend who has lived here longer.

> *"Remember that anyone you hire will learn a great deal about you, including your relative wealth, how to get access to your home, the value of your belongings, and your schedule."*

Never hire anyone who simply knocks on your door and seems to be desperate, hoping you'll feel sorry for them. Local people who are good and honest don't resort to that since they have extended families that have their own connections.

And don't hire people from ads or postings. Only trust word of mouth recommendations from people you trust. Remember that anyone you hire will learn a great deal about you, including your relative wealth, how to get access to your home, the value of your belongings, and your schedule.

These same guidelines apply to general handymen, too. Your landlord or agency will know whom to trust. Plus, there are recommendations on the local online web boards (see Appendix).

There are documents you need to ask for before hiring anyone. The first document is the worker's identification, their national voting credential from the Instituto Federal Electoral (IFE or INE), which everyone has. Then they should have an original (not a copy) of a recent utility bill. That will establish where they live. And then you should get a police clearance letter confirming that they have no criminal history. That costs about 100 pesos. It's available from the Jalisco Institute of Forensic Sciences on the right side of the mercado at the Chapala plaza, right next to Jose's restaurant. There, the person has to have their CURP number, give a thumb print, and have their picture taken. You could even offer to reimburse the 100 pesos for them.

What do I do? I don't mess with any of that. I hire a cleaning service. Then I don't have to worry about sick time or bonus pay. And, it's really inexpensive. I pay the cleaner a nice bonus, too, so everybody's happy. The whole house is ready in four hours for 350 pesos. That's under $20 USD. There are few of these services around, but the one I use is Spring Clean (bit.ly/2vZC3Ob).

Pets

The Lake Chapala area has everything you need for your pets. There are lovely parks to walk your dog in, like Cristiania Park in Chapala, and the various *malecónes* along the coast. The only problems you'll find are the stray dogs that hang out in these areas. They won't necessarily cause any problems, because they're quite well socialized to other dogs and people. It's just that they tend to follow other dogs that they like. So, it can be a nuisance. At worst, you may have to cut your walk short and find another spot.

There are various animal shelters and outreach programs in the area that take homeless, abused, and injured animals off the streets, and try to prepare them for adoption. They're wonderful organizations—usually non-profits—worthy of charitable contributions, if you're so inclined. Despite their best efforts, you will still see some very scruffy dogs on the streets. Some have homes, and some simply live on the streets. In some areas, butchers (*carnicerías*) provide them with daily scraps, and the dogs line up like school-children there for their handouts.

Regarding pet health care, there are plenty of very competent English-speaking veterinarians all along the *carretera*. See here for an article comparing some of them: bit.ly/2wicNH9. You will also find very good pet foods, including north of the border brands at the *supermercados*, and at pet stores. You'll even find high-end brands like Science Diet, IAMS, and specialty diets in some pet stores, like the Animal Shelter A.C. Pet Store in Riberas Del Pilar at 212 Hidalgo (the *carretera*) between Calle San Lucas and Calle San Mateo. That store also carries good flea and tick repellents like Frontline Plus.

As for grooming, there are excellent pet services here, and they're much less expensive than north of the border—about 170 pesos (a little over $10 USD) for an average sized dog. Recommendations can be found on the local web boards. Lots of veterinarians do grooming, too. I prefer going there because then my dogs get a good looking over each time, too.

Cooking

One of the reasons the Lake Chapala area has such a temperate climate (as opposed to the Mexican coasts, which can be hot and humid) is that it is situated high in the mountains—5,000 feet above sea level—about the same as Denver. But for that reason, you may need to adjust the way you cook and bake. High-altitude cooking is the opposite of pressure cooking. The boiling point of water is lower because there is less air pressure, so foods that are boiled will need longer cooking times since they're using a lower temperature. Similarly for baking, liquids evaporate faster since it takes less heat for water to start boiling. In addition, leavening agents like yeast expand faster. Here's an informative website for high-altitude baking: highaltitudebaking.com.

Mail Services

The Mexican government, like every other country's government, provides postal services. From my own experiences and from the other expats I've talked to, they do a pretty good job. Postal carriers, usually on motorcycles, will put your envelopes and flyers (very few of these, thank goodness) in your mailbox, or slide them under your door Monday through Saturday. For packages, they will give you a slip of paper indicating that a box is waiting for you at the post office, and it will have the address of the post office on it.

So, why would you need mail services aside from that? The primary reason is that, because of customs at the border, it takes about two weeks for letters and packages from north of the border to arrive from the time it was sent. So, if you buy something from eBay, for instance (making sure the seller ships to Mexico), you'll have to wait for them to process the order and ship it, and then you'll have to wait 2 weeks for it to be delivered. That could easily mean a wait of 3 weeks. The reverse is true, too. It takes about 2 weeks for items to reach the US and Canada.

If the company you're buying something from north of the border does not ship to Mexico, then you'll want to have a north of the border address. You can, of course, use the address of a friend or family member, who then has to take the time to re-wrap the package, re-address the package, and then go to a post office to ship it to your address here. You probably would not want to ask them to do that for you very often. And, they may not be as speedy as you'd like in getting that done.

So, instead, a mail service here can provide that function for you. You'll be given a post office box in Texas to which your mail, including packages, can be delivered. The mail services' agents there in Texas take your mail though customs, and deliver it to your mail service outlet here, from which you can pick it up. If it's regular first class mail, it takes about the same time as it would if it were sent directly to you. The advantage is that the sender only has to ship it to Texas, and only has to pay for it going that far. That means you can still get your magazines and newspaper subscriptions, if you want, since they don't normally deliver across borders. You end up paying for the rest of the trip, though, and for any customs duties, and for the service when you pick up the items.

Other reasons to use mail services is that they can provide you with a post office box, they often have shipping materials, and they use public and private carriers, like USPS, UPS, DHL, and FedEx.

Here is an article that compares the local mail service companies: bit.ly/2fpsuSk.

Garbage Pickup

Each town has its own garbage pickup services, and they're free—being paid for by taxes. Garbage is picked up every other day in some towns, every day in others, and once a week in others. Everything except very large items seems to be picked up, including yard waste. Most people just put out their plastic bags by the curb. But, in areas where there are street dogs, some people use plastic trash cans, or they hang the bags from tree limbs. You'll want to just follow what your neighbors do in this regard.

You'll also want to consider separating recyclables from regular garbage. If you don't separate them, some locals will actually go through your trash themselves, and pick out the cans and bottles for redemption at the recycle centers. The garbage collectors do that, too, on the trucks.

Beauty Salons and Barbers

For women, there are lots of beauty salons which offer all the hair, nail, and spa services you're used to north of the border. You'll find that the quality of the services is very good, and that every shop has at least one person who speaks English. The prices are lower than comparable services north of the border by at least half. You'll see some salons along the *carretera*, but there are many others interspersed within the towns, as well.

Men can also use these salons, of course, but there are also many traditional barbershops called *peluquerias*.

Tipping is customary for all the services—between 10 and 15%. To find good recommendations for these services, check the web boards (see Appendix).

Chapter 9

Utilities

Your home utilities at Lakeside are fairly straightforward, once you know how they work.

Gas

The simplest of the household utilities is gas for cooking and water heating. Because there is no underground gas pipe system, every house has its own gas tank—usually on the roof. This is replenished, when requested, by independent services that come to your house and fill up the tank. The gas trucks are easy to find since they make regular rounds in the neighborhoods, usually with music playing. You may want to ask your landlord or previous house owner who provided the services in the past, and whether they recommend continuing with that company. When you first move in, you'll want to have someone check the gas level in the tank to make sure you're not about to run out. Actually, if you are renting through a rental agency, ask if they have filled up the tank for you (they should have) so you don't have to take a cold shower on

> *"When you first move in, you'll want to have someone check the gas level in the tank to make sure you're not about to run out."*

your first morning. Compared with electricity at Lakeside, gas is very inexpensive. If you have a choice of gas or electric appliances, like clothes dryers or stoves or even portable heaters, choose the gas ones.

Water

Unless you have a well, your household water is piped in from your town. But it isn't pumped in 24 hours per day due to cost constraints. It's usually pumped in starting in the early morning until mid-afternoon. It goes into a cistern (*aljibe*) on your property, where it stays until the roof-top water tank (*tinaco*) gets low, at which time a pump starts pumping water from the cistern to the water tank to replenish it. For that reason, you'll want to do your laundry and lawn watering early in the day rather than later. The water pressure in your house is

> *"Your tap water is not considered potable (drinkable) no matter how clean the water was when it was piped in from the town."*

(usually) based on gravity from the water falling from the roof-top tank, so you'll find that the water pressure from your taps, shower, and washing machine is less than what you're used to north of the border. Some homes have water pressure pumps, though, which increase the pressure to what you would consider normal levels.

Since this way of receiving and storing water is not a closed system, your tap water is not considered potable (drinkable) no matter how clean the water was when it was piped in from the town—unless you also have a water purification system installed. Both the cistern and the water tank need to be cleaned every six months to a year, and filters replaced, in any case. You can also add chlorine tablets to the cistern, if you'd like.

If you rent your house, this maintenance is usually scheduled and paid for by your landlord. The water itself is also usually paid for by the landlord so you won't be tempted to skimp on watering the garden. Water is actually fairly inexpensive at Lakeside. If you own your home, check with the previous owner regarding system maintenance and water billing from the town. You can also research various places that can install water purification systems and/or water pressure systems in your house. The local web boards (see the Appendix) have very good information on these.

Electricity

Based on the cost of living in Mexico, electricity is considered fairly expensive, and most people (both expats and locals) minimize its use whenever possible. For instance, compact fluorescent (CFL) spiral light bulbs are used much more frequently here than north of the border. There are some types whose light spectrum is quite warm and cozy now. There does not seem to be a shortage of electricity. Outages do occur, but usually only during severe storms or utility pole accidents, and then usually not for long.

Electric plugs are exactly the same as north of the border, with both 2-prong and 3-prong wall plates, so foreign adapters are not needed. The voltage is not consistently at 120, though, sometimes spiking to 140. Surge protectors, while useful for shutting off electricity when there are spikes, do not regulate the voltage. Only voltage regulators can do that, but few people use them because they're costly. At a minimum, you'll want to use surge protectors for your technical devices, which are easy to find and inexpensive here.

The CFE (*Comisión Federal de Electricidad*) is a government-owned utility, and it sends an electric bill every two months to either you or your landlord. The amount charged is based on how much you use according to your house's electric meter readings, just like north of the border. There are three rate levels for home use (*doméstico*). If you exceed an accumulated 3,000 kilowatt hours any time between January and December, your classification will change from a *doméstico* to a DAC (*De Alto Consumo*), and you will have to pay much more. That's because the government subsidizes all *domésticos* by about

> *"Electric plugs are exactly the same as north of the border, with both 2-prong and 3-prong wall plates, so adapters are not needed. The voltage is not consistently at 120, though, sometimes spiking to 140."*

75%. As an example, my own electric bill shows I consumed 373 kilowatt hours, and that the cost of production was 1,711 pesos (about $95 USD for two months). The government paid the first 1,207 pesos (about $67 USD) for me, so my final bill came to 504 pesos (about $28 USD) for two months. That's very inexpensive by my standards, but for some locals, that's plenty.

Homes that have water purification systems, swimming, pools, and water pressure pumps, as well as air conditioning in summer and portable electric heaters in the winter are the ones who tend to reach the DAC level, and thereby lose their subsidy. What some people do to avoid that is to change the account name to their spouse half-way through the year. That resets the counter back to zero. If the DAC level has been reached, though, it will stay that way until 3 two-month bills (6 months' worth) show a lower use consistent with the *doméstico* level. The account will then be considered a *doméstico* again, and the subsidy will be applied.

Solar Energy

The green movement is in full swing at Lakeside, so solar energy is starting to be used here now. There are several companies in the area. You'll want to check the local web boards and my website (see the Appendix) for their names and reviews. Solar energy may make financial sense only if you own your home, and if you plan to stay for a long time, in order to recoup the initial investment. Here's an article on how to tell when the time is right: bit.ly/2yewsou.

Chapter 10

Technology

Advanced technologies for land-line phones, cell phones, TV, internet, personal computers, smart phones, and tablets are all here at Lakeside. As you can imagine, this is where your life can get very complicated. Unlike most of the offerings north of the border, some of the technology choices here don't work very well—or not as well as you'd expect. As a newcomer, you can spend months fuming and switching services until you get just the right mix of what you want. To minimize that as much as possible, here are a few tips.

Land-Line Phone
If your home came with a land-line phone (i.e., wired from the street, you probably have Telmex service (telmex.com). That's the standard Mexican fixed-line carrier. It's a privately owned company (Carlos Slim), but it's fairly close to being a national monopoly. If you decide to remove your Telmex service, they will not only disconnect you electronically at the switching station, they'll come and physically remove the wires, as well. Most people don't want that, for fear that switching back to Telmex might take a long time because of the wiring, and because there may not be available ports at that time. Starting service for a brand new home does take awhile, too, for that reason. The good news is that the Telmex phone service is pretty good. You can have the service options you're used to

north of the border, as well, like call forwarding, call waiting, and voicemail. I haven't experienced or heard of any dial-tone or dropped-call complaints. You can get different plans, of course, for a variety of prices, and they're fairly inexpensive. You do have to watch your phone bill carefully, though, because they sneak in opt-out services occasionally that you didn't ask for, like odd insurance premiums. Do question anything that changes the standard monthly billing amount.

The phone plans that include internet service (bundled packages) have recently been enhanced to include free calls to the US, Canada, and many other countries. And, by law, there are no long-distance charges for any inter-Mexico calls.

Internet

Telmex also offers internet services—both dial-up and DSL (called Infinitum). If you're not too fussy about internet speed, these would be good choices. Although they offer very high-speed service to many large metropolitan areas in Mexico (Guadalajara, Mexico City), the maximum in the area is 5 Mbps to 10 Mbps depending on how far away from a server you are. There have been many complaints about this, but it probably boils down to this area not having enough people (yet) to make it worthwhile to upgrade their equipment.

Another provider of internet service is Telecable (telecable.net.mx). They used to offer speeds of 5, 8, 10, and 15 Mbps, and the actual speed often exceeded these numbers. But, now they say they only provide the 5 Mpbs speed, and only in certain areas. They're the only cable company in the area, but they have an inconsistent record. Sometimes the service drops, and you just have to wait until it comes back online. They offer packages which also includes TV (see below).

There is now one other internet provider that is gaining in popularity. It's a private company called Spiderweb (bit.ly/2wxyTRa). It doesn't work in all areas because it requires a line-of-sight to their tower on the south side of the lake. But they will come to your house and determine if it is eligible. If so, and if you want decent, reliable internet service, they're the ones I recommend. You just buy as many Mpbs as you want. They have a customer here who gets 50 Mpbs. Here's an article with additional information: bit.ly/2xGKen4.

"Be aware that when you get internet service in Mexico, you may no longer be able to view internet content that is copyrighted only for the US and Canadian market."

Be aware that when you get internet service in Mexico, you may no longer be able to view internet content that is copyrighted only for the US and Canadian market. And, a good deal of the content will be automatically translated into Spanish for you. That's because you will have a Mexican IP address for your computer, which the internet sites read in order to determine where you are, what they can show you, and in what language. For example, if you go to Netflix, you'll only see the shows authorized to be shown in Mexico. Some sites may not be available at all, like Hulu Plus or Vudu.

There are some ways to make websites think you're in the US, though. Here is a good article summarizing your options: bit.ly/2f1yKPu.

Sometimes, however, you will want to switch back to your Mexican IP address because some sites actually require that you not be in the US. One of these is USTVNow (see the section on TV).

And some sites, like iTunes, are tricky. They don't use your IP address to determine your location. They use your billing credit card's address. Mine happens to be Mexican. So, it assumes I'm in Mexico, and will only show me titles authorized to be distributed in Mexico (there are fewer of them). And, all the iTunes pages are in Spanish, too. So, this is another reason to keep at least one US credit card alive and funded.

Radio

There is very little of interest that's loud enough to hear on traditional radio here at Lakeside. That includes both FM and AM. The problem is not that there are no stations playing, it's that the reception is poor due to the surrounding mountains.

Your car radio will be almost useless in this area, except for the speakers for playing your favorite music or podcasts from your portable devices using Bluetooth or USB.

TV

I don't recommend buying a complete phone-internet-TV bundle from Telecable because they don't offer a phone voicemail service, which they don't tell you about up front. Their TV service is a mixed bag. The US broadcast channels like NBC are copied off US's DISH satellite, and often look like they're copied: a low quality picture. So, I would only recommend the internet service from Telecable.

There are other satellite network TV offerings here that are pretty reliable—including HD (High Definition). Shaw Network is very well liked, but you have to buy a receiver and a large satellite dish. It's a Canadian company, but the equipment can be purchased in Guadalajara at CP Electronics (bit.ly/2xq5ZGB). Check the local web boards for more information about this option, and to inquire about used equipment and service plans.

SKY satellite network is also good. They will come and install the dish free of charge if you sign an 18 month contract. They have various package deals with various channel groupings, many of which have US channels and premium channels. There's a good mixture of Mexican and US channels available. Be aware though, that US media companies have different programming for Mexico. You're not necessarily going to get first-run programming on HBO, for instance. SKY just airs whatever HBO chooses to send them, which may or may not be what people in the US are seeing. Sometimes the CNN channel broadcasts CNN US, and sometimes it broadcasts CNN International. And the Fox station plays a lot of The Simpsons reruns. Basically, you get what you get.

> *"Be aware, though, that US media companies have different programming for Mexico."*

Regarding payments, you can have SKY automatically charge your monthly fee to your credit card, but they won't accept debit cards, except over the phone. With all these caveats, I still find SKY a good choice for me. Their website is sky.com.mx, and their English-speaking phone number for customers is 800-475-9759.

The DirecTV Mexico satellite network is available here, but it has mostly Spanish channels. The US DirecTV offerings used to be available only in the US, but since they've switched satellites, it's now possible to get reception Lakeside, although you'll need to get assistance with the equipment requirements. Assistance can be found on the web boards (see the Appendix), where at least a few satellite tech people tune in.

The DISH Mexico (dishmexico.com) satellite network is also available here. You'll want to compare its offerings with the others. I suspect it's similar to SKY, but I haven't tried it because I was so disappointed with the quality of the local US channels that Telecable offered via DISH. Again, you'll want to find out whether the channels (like Fox, HBO, and CNN) air the same streams that are shown in the US, or whether the streams consist mostly of reruns. You'll also want to ask whether programming schedules are available. And, you'll want to find out which channels are in Spanish, which are in English, which are in Spanish with English subtitles, and which are in English with Spanish subtitles. You'll probably find, as I unexpectedly did, that you'll come to appreciate programming in English with Spanish subtitles to help you learn Spanish.

There are many live-streaming US (and maybe Canadian) TV channels available on the internet, both nationally broadcast channels, as well as cable. The one I use is USTVNow (ustvnow.com). You can get the basic package for free, which includes ABC, CBS, CW, FOX, NBC, and PBS. You have to have a non-US IP address in order for it to work. There are also fee-based packages that include cable stations and HD—and even a DVR function for the channels. You have to have a fairly fast (I recommend at least 5MB) internet service, though, for this to be useful. Otherwise, the video will spend more time getting hung up than playing. There are also live streaming options of various US-based channels, like Fox and CNN and MSNBC. Just Google "live streaming" and your favorite channel to see the options.

Cell Phone

When you first move to Lake Chapala, you can use your existing north of the border cell phone, using its roaming feature for both voice and text messaging. But you'll want to turn that feature off except when you're actually using it because it's expensive. It's not just expensive when you're using it, it's expensive when you're not using it if you have the phone in stand-by mode because cell phones communicate a great deal with their providers—updating location information and applications, and monitoring minutes left.

Because of the expense of continually using a north-of-the-border cell phone, you'll want to research your best option for getting a Mexican one—either as a replacement, or as an additional one. The five main cell phone carriers in this area are:

- Telcel
- Unefon
- Movistar
- IUSACELL

- AT&T

Cell phone calls all go through Guadalajara, which is why they have different city codes than land phones here (see the Index for Telephone Dialing).

Some people swear by each of the above carriers, so which one to choose is really a matter of personal preference, including who has the best service plan for voice and data at the time, who gets the best reception in which areas, who has an area-wide 3G and 4G network, who is using GSM, and who bundles your favorite phone into the plan. Because these factors change over time, my advice is to look on the local web boards (see the Appendix) for the most up-to-date information.

Telcel has an advantage in that it has a huge customer service center in the big Centro Laguna Mall across from Walmart. There are English speakers there, and they'll even help you if you're confused about a certain cell phone feature. They have phone technicians there, too, for fixing basic phone problems.

Some carriers, like Telcel, offer you plans (usually without having to sign a long contract) for various levels of calls and data per month, or you can just pay as you go. Air time can be purchased in most stores if you don't have a plan.

I do not recommend using any of the smaller Telcel shops in the area. Some find ways of short-changing their customers. See here for an article about this: bit.ly/2ha0QZJ.

By the way, if you haven't subscribed to a monthly plan, if you receive a call on your Mexican cell phone, you'll be charged. Both the sender and the receiver pay.

The decision around cell phones can make you crazy in a hurry, if you let it, because the options and the specials and the plans and the phones change frequently. Dare to opt for "good enough."

Smart Phones and Tablets

As with most electronics, you'll pay a lower price in the US because of the customs fees vendors have to pay to get them imported to Mexico. Plus, there's a 16% sales tax in Mexico. So, it's generally wiser to bring your electronics with you when you move to this area unless you're moving from somewhere other than north of the border. Also, be aware that Mexican keyboards have a different layout than English keyboards. There are computer technicians in the area that can help convert the keyboard, though, using stickers and making some software changes. In general, though, it's best to just buy an English device.

> *"Also, be aware that Mexican computer keyboards have a different layout than English keyboards."*

Smart phones and tablets are really small computers, so everything noted in the section above regarding the internet applies to these devices, too. That is, the internet will know you're in Mexico unless you use a service or router that hides your true location by masking your IP address. And, the speed of the internet and emailing will depend on the speed of the internet service you sign up for through Telecable or TelMex or Spiderweb.

Chapter 11

Banking

As with the technology sector, the banking industry Lakeside is not quite what you are used to north of the border. They seem to have the technology, but it isn't as stable, and they are not as focused on the customer experience as they are north of the border

As mentioned earlier, you'll want to keep at least one north-of-the-border credit card as a backup, at least for awhile, until you're confident about your new Mexican banking arrangements. Or permanently. There's no downside to using your north of the border credit card, except that you'll have to keep remembering the north of the border address and phone number that you used to open up that credit card account with every time you use it as a "billing address" online. By the way, check with your credit card provider to find out whether they charge an international usage fee. One that I'm aware of that does not charge it is CapitalOne. You may want to research that as one of your options.

If you have a PayPal account, you may want to keep that open, too, for north of the border online purchases through Amazon and eBay. The reason for that is that the debit card you will get from a Lakeside bank may or may not work online.

There are many major banks here, including HSBC, Banamex, Bancomer, CI Banco, Santander, and ScotiaBank. Bank of America has some arrangements with both Santander and ScotiaBank that may be worth investigating. There are also investment companies locally. Of these, I would not recommend Banamex. Their systems seem to be the least stable, and their customer service leaves a lot to be desired. Based on my personal experiences, I would recommend either Bancomer or HSBC.

With the tax and finance laws implemented in 2014, anyone who opens a new bank account must have an RFC number (Registro Federal de Contribuyentes). It's a taxpayer number assigned by the SAT (Mexico's tax agency) so they can keep track of money flow, which is especially important with the recent passing of anti-money laundering laws. In order to get an RFC number, though, you must first have a CURP number, which is a national identification number. As a newcomer, you will probably want someone to get these for you since they require applications in Spanish and separate government offices. The following law office provides this service for a fee:

Spencer McMullen
Hidalgo #230 (the *carretera*)
Chapala
Phone: 376-765-7553

Again, there is no reason why you can't use only your own north-of-the-border bank's services and credit/debit cards here, thereby avoiding any need to deal with a Mexican bank. You can withdraw money from an ATM here at a good exchange rate. The ATM fees for credit card cash withdrawals vary widely. One of the lowest fees is at CI Banco's ATM in the Centro Laguna Mall in San Antonio.

Aside from fees, other downsides to using only north-of-the-border credit cards are:
1. You won't have an opportunity to build a Mexican credit history. But, that may not be of much importance to you.
2. You can only withdraw up to a certain daily limit from an ATM. That's usually around $700 USD.
3. You can do a wire transfer from your north of the border bank to places at Lakeside (like banks or at Walmart), but you'll be charged a transfer fee of around $15 USD.

Speaking of ATMs, you'll want to use the ATM at your bank's location whenever possible since it has the least possibility of being tampered with. Also, do withdraw enough cash from your ATM on Fridays to cover you through the weekend, since some of the ATMs run out of cash before Monday morning.

By the way, you may not use a cell phone in a bank. This includes both placing a call and answering a call. If your cell phone rings in a bank, just turn it off. You may not answer it. This rule is to prevent someone inside a bank from tipping off someone outside the bank when a patron withdraws a large amount of money.

Mexican bank accounts are secured by a government organization similar to USA's FDIC (Federal Deposit Insurance Corporation). It's called IPAB, and the current savings protection is up to 1.9 million pesos per account. The website is here: ipab.org.mx

There's also a government agency called CONDUSEF, through which you can file a complaint against a Mexican financial institution. Its website is condusef.gob.mx. This agency is very powerful, and can convince a bank that it's in its best financial interest to settle a claim.

Chapter 12

Government Services

You will most likely come into contact with many government services at Lakeside. Most of them are staffed with at least one English-speaker. With a little preparation on your part, these services will be of great benefit to you.

Visas

A new Mexican immigration law became effective in 2012, which affected expats significantly. Previously, residence visas could be applied for within Mexico, and some visas could be renewed indefinitely. That is no longer the case.

There are really four aspects of immigration:

- what the *law* actually states
- what the law's associated *regulations* actually state
- what neither of them state (what is open to interpretation)
- how each immigration or consulate office (and sometimes each agent) chooses to implement the law and regulations.

The lengthy new immigration law itself is complete. There is nothing intentionally left out. However, the law often references associated regulations for implementation of the law, some of which have never been published. However, there is now enough experience and case history to understand how the system generally works in this region.

Tourist Card (FMM)

Whether you drive across the border to Mexico, or you fly in, you will be able to get a Tourist card (it's not really considered a visa) at the border or aboard the plane. That's true only if you're coming from a travel-visa-waiver country. No income qualifications are needed. Don't sign up for tourist status, though, if you already have (or have started) a temporary or permanente resident visa. It will invalidate that other visa or visa process.

> *"Don't sign up for tourist status, though, if you already have (or have started) a temporary or permanente resident visa. It will invalidate that other visa or visa process."*

You can be a tourist for up to 180 days, and then go back across the border and renew it immediately for another 180 days. There's no waiting time between renewals. And, in theory, you could do that forever. But, that might become restricted in the future if immigration decides that too many people are just skirting the financial requirements of getting a visa. It's true, you don't have to worry about qualifying for a longer-term visa by

> *"You can only apply for a residence visa in your home country's Mexican consulate."*

remaining a tourist, but you also don't get the benefits of having a longer-term visa, like being able to open a Mexican bank account (although a few banks now make exceptions), qualifying for Seguro Popular or IMSS health insurance, getting a worker's permit, and getting a senior discount card like DIF and INAPAM. You can, however, buy real estate on a Tourist card.

Most importantly, the law states that you can no longer upgrade from a Tourist card to a longer-term visa from within Mexico—with very few exceptions. Significant exceptions are if you have close family ties in Mexico such as a spouse or children who are Mexican citizens. In those cases, you can apply for a visa while in Mexico on a Tourist card.

Whenever you leave Mexico, you will turn in your Tourist card. If you came in by car, though, and decide to fly out, immigration agents may give you problems. They want you to drive your car back out, not fly out, because they're trying to prevent people from dumping their old cars in Mexico, which has become a big problem.

Residente Temporal Visa
If you're going to be in Mexico longer than 180 days, you may want to apply for a Residente Temporal or a Residente Permanente visa. But, **you can only apply for a residence visa in your home country's Mexican consulate**. If you're retired, you have to prove one of the following

qualifications (based on a conversion rate of 18 pesos to the US dollar).

- 6 months bank statements showing *average* monthly income of 24,010 pesos or **$1,334 USD** (300 days minimum wage) – can come from either employment or pension.
- <u>or</u> 12 months bank statements showing investment savings of an *average* of 400,166 pesos or **$22,232 USD** (5,000 days minimum wage)

Mexican consulates north of the border do not all apply the law and regulations the same way. For most of them, these financial qualifications apply to *each adult*, whether married or not. So, if you're part of a couple, you may want to visit your Mexican consulate to find out what their requirements are in advance (or check their website) if you're concerned about both of you qualifying. You may need to sign over some financial accounts to your partner six or twelve months before applying so *you can both qualify*. As a last resort, you may want to try applying at either the Las Vegas, Nevada or the Laredo, Texas Mexican consulates. They are quite lenient in their requirements.

If you're not retired, and you work for a company (Mexican or foreign), the company can assist you in getting a worker's permit attached to your Residente Temporal visa. Be aware, though, that the visa will expire as soon as your employment with that company ends unless you're immediately hired by another company. If you're not retired (with an independent income) and not working for a company that can help you get a worker's permit, you will not be able to legally work in Mexico to earn a living (unless you qualify for a Residente Permanente visa or become a Mexican citizen). Your best bet will be to stick with a renewable Tourist card and take your chances on (illegally) earning a living. You won't be the only one to have done this.

If you already have a Residente Temporal visa, you can apply for a worker's permit from within Mexico, though (you will need an attorney or facilitator for this). You will only be approved if it looks like you'll be hiring Mexican workers, or at least not taking jobs away from Mexican workers or competing with them. Or, you could qualify as having unique skills, such as being an artist, photographer, or writer. But then, that's how your income has to be earned, too.

If the Mexican consulate in your home country approves your application for a Residente Temporal visa, you will get a special visa sticker on your passport. Then you will have 6 months to enter Mexico. When entering Mexico, you will need to fill out an FMM document, but instead of indicating that you're a tourist, you should indicate "Canje" (on item #8 below) and show the visa sticker the consulate placed in your passport. Here's a sample document:

Living at Lake Chapala: Government Services

Show the agents your FMM document so they can fill out their parts, and then you will have 30 days to have that exchanged for an actual visa card at your local Mexican immigration office. It may take some weeks to actually get your new card. If you need to leave Mexico before you have your card, you'll need a travel letter. It's best to see an immigration facilitator or lawyer for one of these.

Your home consulate will probably only give you approval for a 1-year visa. About one month before your visa expires, you can go to your local immigration office in Mexico to have it renewed for either 1, 2, or 3 more years. The current renewal cost is 3,715, 5,567, or 7,050 pesos, respectively, not counting facilitator fees. The maximum total amount of time you will have on your Residente Temporal visa is 4 years. There are no restrictions on how long you can be out of the country during those 4 years.

> *"Your home consulate will probably only give you approval for a 1-year visa."*

After the 4th year of having a Residente Temporal visa with no renewal lapses or expirations, you can apply locally for a Residente Permanente visa *without* having to prove any more financial qualifications. You can simply slide in. If you received your temporary visa before the new immigration law came into effect (November of 2012), the years you've had a temporary visa (some timely-renewed combination of the old FM2, FM3, or Residente Temporal visas) will probably be taken into account in order to qualify you.

But, if you do not qualify for becoming a Residente Permanente in this way (by sliding in), and you don't qualify for a Residente Permanente visa based on your financial qualifications, you will need to leave the country after the 4 years. You can go back to your home country and apply for a new Residente Temporal visa. Of course, you will have to show proof of the then-prevailing financial requirements. If that doesn't work, you could still enter Mexico as a tourist.

Residente Permanente Visa

If you haven't had 4 years on an uninterrupted (unexpired) temporary visa, enabling you to slide into a Residente Permanente visa, there are three ways to get a Residente Permanente visa:

- Apply for it from your home country's Mexican consulate, if you meet the required financial requirements (see below).
- If you already have a Residente Temporal visa, you can jump ahead to a Residente Permanente visa by qualifying financially. This can be done either from within Mexico or from your home country's Mexican consulate.
- Marry a Mexican citizen or be closely related to one (like your child). You can apply for the visa from

within Mexico or your home country's Mexican consulate.

Having a Residente Permanente visa confers more Mexican benefits, like never having to renew the visa, and being able to earn an income without a permit. It's not citizenship, but it's close. If you qualify for a Residente Permanente visa at your home country's consulate, the document you will get is a Canje FMM, just like the one shown above, and a visa sticker on your passport.

> *"Residente Permanentes may not import a foreign-plated vehicle."*

However, there is what many expats consider a limitation: Residente Permanentes may not import a foreign-plated vehicle. If you're part of couple, it may make sense for one of you to remain a Residente Temporal for this reason (both of you can still drive it). Before the new law, it was a toss-up whether to sell your car north of the border before coming to Mexico or not. That's because temporary visas were easy to renew in Mexico indefinitely. Now, it's best to sell your car north of the border if you plan to become a Residente Permanente. You will have four years to think about it, of course.

If you're retired, the financial requirements to become a Residente Permanente are:

- 6 months bank statements showing *average* monthly income of 40,020 pesos (**$2,223 USD** at exchange rate 18). That's 500 times the daily minimum wage.
- or 12 months bank statements showing investment savings of an *average* of 1,600,800 pesos (**$88,933 USD** at exchange rate 18). That's 20,000 times the daily minimum wage.
- or having an *unexpired* temporary visa for 4 years (some combination of the old FM2, FM3, and Residente Temporal visas).

According to the *law*, there is one other condition: having a minimum score on a points system. The point system is one of those regulations that never got published—and it may never get published. Just as for the Residente Temporal visa, there are no restrictions on how long you can be out of the country if you have a Residente Permanente visa.

If you want to go further, you can apply for Mexican citizenship after 5 years as a Residente Permanente (unless you qualify sooner for any other reason), in which case you'll have voting rights, too, plus permission to get involved in Mexican politics (signing petitions, running for office, etc.).

Local Mexican immigration offices vary somewhat in the types of documents they require for one thing or another, and in how long they take to make something happen.

INAPAM and DIF Senior Discount Cards

One of the benefits of obtaining a residence visa, either Residente Temporal or Residente Permanente, is that you can get two free senior discount cards if you're over 60. The INAPAM organization is like the federal government's version of the US's AARP (American Association of Retired Persons), and the card is just one of the benefits the organization offers.

You can get 10% – 15% off participating movie theaters, and 50% off buses, including both the local buses Lakeside and bus tours. It's also good at some airlines, at Guadalajara's zoo, at the Walmart pharmacy, and at Farmácia Guadalajara. There are three of these pharmacies on the *carretera*—one in Chapala near the Villa Montecarlo Hotel, one in Ajijic at the corner of Guerra street, and one in Jocotepec.

The DIF card is similar to the INAPAM card, except that it's run by the state's social services department rather than the federal government. Some places take one or the other or both. It never hurts to ask your merchants if they honor them. You will be surprised how many of them do.

If you're planning to go on a bus trip, be aware that there are only a certain number of DIF/INAPAM seats available per trip. So, you'll want to purchase your tickets in advance to ensure you get one of the discounted seats.

Both cards are permanent; they never need to be renewed.

Here is where to get both cards in Chapala.

DIF/INAPAM Office
Degollado #327, Chapala
Phone Number: 376-765-3349

Directions : Going toward Chapala on the *carretera*, turn left at the main Madero stoplight. Turn right two blocks north of the plaza (Degollado). Continue on Degollado (you will cross Juarez, Zaragoza, and 5 de Mayo). The building is on your left in the middle of the following block next to the Chapala post office.

You need to bring:
- the original and 2 copies of your old-style FM-3 or FM-2 card, or of your new Residente Temporal or Residente Permanente card. Make sure each copy has an image of the front and the back of the card on the same page.
- your passport and 2 copies of the photo and signature page.
- 4 *infantile*-size (small) color photos of yourself. You must be facing forward.
- a recent proof of residence document. This can be an electric or water bill, or a Telmex or TV service bill, like Telecable. If you don't have one of these in your own name, they'll take one in your landlord's name.
- your blood type. A simple blood test taken at any laboratory for about 150 pesos can inform you of this, if you don't know it. They don't require proof.

Driver's License

You must have an unexpired driver's license if you drive a car in Mexico. The license can be from a foreign country, though. Check with your home country to find out if yours can be renewed by mail. If not, it's time to get a Mexican driver's license, as long as you have a residence visa. If you don't, you'll have to return to your home country to have it renewed, or face a stiff fine if you're caught driving without a valid license.

You will have to get a CURP (*Clave Única de Registro de Población*) document from the immigration office before applying for your Mexican driver's license. It has an 18-character identity number that both Mexicans and residents need for a number of things (bank accounts, worker's permits, and government health insurance, for instance). Here's an article with more information about CURP numbers: bit.ly/2xbosGm. A lawyer or immigration facilitator can help you get a CURP number, if you'd rather have someone else do it.

You used to be able to get a driver's license in Chapala. That's no longer the case. It's best now to see a facilitator or lawyer for the current procedure and location.

The requirements to get a Mexican driver's license are:

- You must be 18 years of age or older.
- You must bring your passport and one black & white copy of the face/signature page.

- You must have your residence visa card and one black & white copy.
- You must know your blood type.
- You must have proof of address and one black & white copy. This can be a utility bill, telephone bill, water bill, or a Mexican bank statement, none of which can be more than 90 days old.
- You must have your CURP document (not just the number).
- You must pass a vision test (although this is seldom done).
- You must pass a test on rules of the road.
- You must pass a road test.
- You must pay a fee, if you pass the tests. It's around 600 pesos.

If your utility bill is in someone else's name, like your landlord's, they probably will not accept it here as proof of address (although other places, like banks, usually do). You will instead need a special residence certificate (*certificado de domicilio*) from the Chapala administrative office located in the large red brick building on Madero near the Chapala malecón. They will need to see your utility bill, your rental lease, and your passport. You may have to come back the next day for your certificate, which costs about 50 pesos.

There are no study guides for the test on rules of the road. It's a multiple-choice test using a computer screen showing various images of traffic scenarios. Most of them are common sense. It's in Spanish, but there's an English translator there, if you need one. You can choose to get a regular driver's license or a *chofer* (chauffeur) license. You might as a well choose the *chofer* license because you won't be allowed to drive a pick-up truck without it. The test questions are the same; the only difference is a slightly higher fee.

"You must have your original driver's license with you whenever you drive."

When taking your driving test, make sure you turn on your blinking hazard lights whenever you back up. That's the law in Mexico. And, remember to drive with both hands on the wheel if you're used to driving with only one hand. By the way, you must always have your original driver's license with you whenever you drive. A copy is not good enough, so keep that at home.

Police

There are different classifications of police at Lakeside (in Mexico, actually). The *movilidad* (formerly, but sometimes still called *tránsitos)* are considered the lowest level. They report to the state of Jalisco. They deal only with driving and traffic issues. They're real police, though, with real powers, although they're the least educated (often not having a high school education), and the least paid. Some don't know the driving laws very well. In the past, their salaries were kept low because the custom of taking *mordidas* (bribes) made up for it. This practice is disappearing, but it still exists to some degree. And, expats are assumed to be rich, so we're the perfect targets. Offering and taking bribes is illegal in Mexico, so think carefully about offering it. Your best bet, if you don't want to pay it, is to keep repeating, "*No hablo español*," or pretend you don't know what they're hinting at, or keep insisting that you want the ticket. Most of the time, the bribe will be more than the actual fine, so you're better off insisting on the ticket. Besides, if you pay the ticket within 10 days, the fine is cut in half. And remember, the police cannot confiscate any of your documents, including your driver's license, under any circumstances.

> *"The police cannot confiscate any of your documents, including your driver's license, under any circumstances."*

There's a listing of Jalisco and federal traffic laws on my website at LakeChapalaReporter.com. You may want to keep a copy of them in your glove compartment to show the *movilidad* police what the law really says. If all else fails, call your lawyer's cell phone, whose number you should always have in your cell phone or on the Driving Accident Form in the Appendix. This will prevent the *movilidad* from taking further advantage of you, if that's their intent.

The next level up is the municipal police, called the *policía preventiva*. Their job is to prevent crime within their municipal area, and to record initial crime information. They don't do extensive crime investigations, though. That's done by the state of Jalisco's attorney general's office (*Ministeria Publica*).

Next there's the Jalisco state police force, which reports to the state governor. They're called *Policía Estatales*.

And then there are two classifications of federal police: the *Policía Federal* and the *Policía Federal Ministerial*, whose job it is to conduct investigations. These levels are listed in increasing salary grade levels, so you're less likely to be approached for a *mordida* the higher up the ladder you go. And, lastly, there's the Mexican military, for very serious situations.

There are phone numbers in the Appendix for emergencies, and for reporting any police misconduct.

Passports

If you are an expat in Mexico, you should already have a passport from your home country. Mexico won't let you in without one (with very few exceptions, like for day workers crossing the border repeatedly), and your home country will require one when/if you return. Plus, you will not be able to apply for residence visas without one, or open a bank account, or get senior discount cards. And, you'll have trouble renting a house from a reputable agency, too, without one. Your passport is your primary form of identification here. In fact, you probably won't be allowed to withdraw cash at a bank window without it.

Because it's so important, you don't want to risk losing your passport by carrying it around with you every day. You'll want to have a certified copy made, which you can then keep in your car's glove compartment. Certified copies can only be made by a *Notario Público*. The place I recommend is Notaria 5, located in the orange stucco building at 245-D Hidalgo (that's the *carretera*—the main road) in Chapala. It's in the block just west of the main intersection of Hidalgo and Madero streets. They speak English, and are very easy to work with. The phone number is 376-765-2740.

If you need to renew, replace, or receive a new US passport, here is the US State Department link that can advise you about what you need in order to apply: bit.ly/2fpKETV. And here is the link for Canadian expats: bit.ly/2f2dRnh.

The closest US and Canadian consulates/embassies are in Guadalajara. Their locations are listed in the Appendix. A representative of the US Embassy comes to the Lake Chapala Society once a month. You'll want to contact them to determine the latest schedule at: bit.ly/2h83H8W. A representative also visits the American Legion in Chapala. The legion's website is: bit.ly/2h7xWwO.

Appendix

Exploratory Trip Checklist

Planning your exploratory trip
- ☐ Make sure passport is current.
- ☐ Book flight to Guadalajara airport (5 – 7 day round trip).
- ☐ Book bed and breakfast inn room in Ajijic.
- ☐ Plan transportation from airport to Ajijic.

During your exploratory trip
- ☐ Visit Lake Chapala Society.
- ☐ Buy area maps.
- ☐ Decide whether you want to relocate to Lake Chapala.
- ☐ Find place to live.
- ☐ Establish mailing address for both envelopes and packages.
- ☐ Make arrangements for border driver, if needed.

Move Planning Checklists

Four Weeks Before Moving

- ☐ Set move date.
- ☐ Tell family and friends.
- ☐ Renew passport.
- ☐ Apply for travel visa if Mexico requires one from your home country.
- ☐ Apply for temporary vehicle import permit online, if desired.
- ☐ Decide what to do about pets.
- ☐ Decide what to do about house (or give notice).
- ☐ Decide what to do about car.
- ☐ Decide what to do about belongings.
- ☐ Apply for visa at Mexican consulate (if desired).
- ☐ If coming as Tourist, make sure driver's license is good for 6 months, unless renewable by mail.
- ☐ Meet with accountant or financial advisor.
- ☐ Establish banking plan and new bank account/credit accounts (if desired)
- ☐ Extend health insurance policy to 3 months past planned move date.
- ☐ Get certified copies of marriage license and other important documents (if applicable).
- ☐ Determine if car insurance covers Mexico.

Appendix: Move Planning Checklists

Three Weeks Before Moving

- ☐ Pack last 2 years of health records from doctors, plus dentist x-rays.
- ☐ Switch all statements from hardcopy to online payment.
- ☐ Switch all periodicals from hardcopy to digital.
- ☐ Buy IKEA bags.
- ☐ Get language translation applications and GPS (with Mexican map) for portable electronic devices.
- ☐ Learn how cell phone will behave, and how much it will cost to use in Mexico.
- ☐ Ship books using M-Class.

Two Weeks Before Moving

- ☐ Pack 2 months of medication.
- ☐ Buy pet carriers.
- ☐ Notify post office of change of address (or not).
- ☐ Pack printout of the last 3 months of primary checking account. You may not be able to access printer quickly later.
- ☐ Pack 3 copies of passport photo and signature page, driver's license, car title, and car registration.
- ☐ Take pets to vet, pack 3 copies of their international health certificates.
- ☐ Get car checkup.

One Week Before Moving

- ☐ Pack copy of Jalisco state and Mexico federal driving laws and fines in car's glove compartment.
- ☐ Tell bank and credit card companies that you're going to be in Mexico so they won't decline your "unusual location" transactions.
- ☐ Get haircut and nails done.
- ☐ If driving, bring the equivalent of 10,000 pesos for toll roads, gas, and lodging. Sometimes only cash is accepted, and/or your credit card may be declined due to "unusual location," even if you've notified them in advance.
- ☐ Make final border driver meeting arrangements.

Border Checklist

- ☐ Get an FMM tourist visa (only if you haven't applied for a residence visa).
- ☐ Get a temporary importation vehicle permit (TIP) and sticker (if you didn't get one online)
- ☐ Pass customs.
- ☐ Purchase one month's auto insurance, if you don't already have Mexican auto insurance.

Moving In Checklists

First week
- ☐ Buy bottled water along with food (if needed).
- ☐ Get emergency numbers.
- ☐ Get locks changed.
- ☐ Determine household help names and schedules.
- ☐ Have existing electricity, gas, telephone, and tap water transferred to your name, if possible).
- ☐ Get TV service.
- ☐ Get internet service.
- ☐ Complete house walk-through with agency or landlord.
- ☐ Get name and phone number of handyman.
- ☐ Learn about the maintenance schedule of your gas tank, water tank, and cistern.
- ☐ Learn about garbage collection.
- ☐ Learn about fumigation.
- ☐ Join the Lake Chapala Society.
- ☐ Buy several area maps (car, purse, home).
- ☐ Make spare sets of keys.
- ☐ Choose mailing service.

Appendix: Moving In Checklists

Second week
- ☐ Apply for residence visa card if you have Canje document from home Mexican consulate.
- ☐ Apply for Mexican health insurance.
- ☐ Get Mexican cell phone.

Third week
- ☐ Get annual Mexican auto insurance.
- ☐ Arrange for household help, if needed.

Whenever you can
- ☐ Notify Aduana of new residence visa status, if any, in order to update vehicle importation status.
- ☐ Get CURP and RFC numbers.
- ☐ Open Mexican bank account (if desired).
- ☐ Have important documents notarized.
- ☐ Get DIF and INAPAM senior discount cards.

Recommended Reading

Magazines
- *Lake Chapala Reporter (*online*)*
    I publish this. Check here for book updates, law updates, and articles to keep expats informed.
    LakeChapalaReporter.com
- *El Ojo del Lago* (in print, 5th of every month)
    Available free at local news stands.
    Published by Coldwell Banker Chapala (real estate).
    ojo.chapala.com

Books
- *Baby Boomers: Reinvent Your Retirement in Mexico*
    Karen Blue, 2014
- *How to Live a Caviar Lifestyle on a Tuna Fish Pension: Safe, Beautiful & Affordable Lake Chapala, Mexico*
    Sid Grosvenor, 2013
- *Living at Lake Chapala: Live the Adventure at Lake Chapala*
    Judy King, 2013
- *Mexico's Lake Chapala & Ajijic: The Insider's Guide*
    Teresa A. Kendrik
    Mexico Traveler's Information, 2007

Newspapers
- *Guadalajara Reporter* (in print weekly)
    Available at local news stands

Appendix: Recommended Reading

TheGuadalajaraReporter.com

Facebook Pages and Groups

These are preferable to the Web boards below because they're moderated much better. No trolls or haters tolerated here.

- bit.ly/2wxwExf (Lake Chapala Reporter)
- bit.ly/2xbo6Qg (Guadalajara Reporter)
- bit.ly/2w1AKhw (Ajijic Newbies)
- bit.ly/2yfLg6E (Gringos Ajijic & Lakeside)

Web Boards

- bit.ly/2hazXbx (Chapala com)
    Most popular local web board.
- insidelakeside.com
    Local web board.
- bit.ly/2yftDUm (MexConnect)
    Local web board.

Places and Services

The Lake Chapala Society, A.C.
16 de Septiembre #16-A
Ajijic, Jalisco
Phone: 376-766-1140
LakeChapalaSociety.com
Office open Monday – Saturday from 10 to 2
Grounds open Monday – Saturday from 9 to 5

U.S. Consulate General – Guadalajara
Progreso #175
Colonia Americana
C.P. 44100
Guadalajara, Jalisco
Phone: 333-268-2100
bit.ly/2jyKFcN
Office open Monday - Friday 8 to 4:30

Consulate of Canada - Guadalajara
World Trade Center
Av. Mariano Otero #1249
Piso 8, Torre Pacífico
Col. Rinconada del Bosque
44530 Guadalajara, Jalisco
Phone: 333-671-4740
bit.ly/2fqL2Bw
Office open Monday – Friday 10 to 2

Appendix: Places and Services

For visas and immigration
    SEGOB (*Secretaría de Gobernación Inmigración*)
    271 Hidalgo (*carretera*)
    Chapala, Jalisco
    inm.gob.mx
    Office open Monday – Friday from 9 to 1

For DIF and INAPAM cards
    DIF/INAPAM Office
    Degollado #327, Chapala
    Phone: 376-765-3349
    sn.dif.gob.mx (DIF)   bit.ly/2y6baIY (INAPAM)
    Office open Mondays and Tuesdays from 9 to 2

For taxis
    Ajijic taxi stand (*sitio*) at Plaza
    376-766-0674 or 766-1663
    7am to 8pm

    Chapala taxi stand (*sitio*) at Plaza
    376-765-3511 or 765-4697
    6am to 9pm

Vehicle Accident Form

Fill in the blanks regarding your relevant information so that it is available if you have an accident. Put a copy of this in your car, or have a copy of this book, so you also have the phone numbers of people who can help you.

**Emergency hotline – Lake Chapala area
(Police, Fire, Ambulance)**   **066**

Green Angels (assistance on toll highways)   078

My Mexican telephone numbers:
Home   _____
Cell   _____

Attorney
Name: _____
Office phone: _____
Cell: _____

My insurance adjuster: (At least a telephone #)
_____
_____

My vehicle insurance agent:
_____
Name of insurance company: _____
Policy number: _____

Appendix: Vehicle Accident Form

Emergency contacts:
    Local (neighbor or friend)
    Name: _____
    Phone: _____
    Cell: _____

    Family contact #1:
    Name: _____
    Relationship: _____
    Country: _____
    Country telephone code: _____
    Phone: _____
    Cell: _____

    Family contact #2:
    Name: _____
    Relationship: _____
    Country: _____
    Country telephone code: _____
    Phone: _____
    Cell: _____

At the site of the accident, fill out this form and keep it.

Date:_____
Time:_____

Road conditions:
_____

Traffic conditions:
_____

Weather conditions:
_____

Visibility:
_____

Your vehicle:
Driver's name: _____
Driver's license number: _____
issued by the state/province of
_____
Country:_____
Vehicle license plate number: _____
issued by the state/province of:
_____
Country: _____
Vehicle make: _____
Model: _____
Year: _____

Appendix: Vehicle Accident Form

Other vehicle(s):
Owner's name:

Owner's address:

Owner's telephone number:

Driver's name:

Driver's address:

Driver's telephone number:

Driver's license number:
issued by the state/province of:

Country:
Owner's insurance company, policy number and contact information:

Vehicle license plate number:
issued by the state/province of:

Country: _____
Vehicle make: _____
Model: _____
Year: _____
Witnesses' information:
Names: Telephone numbers:

_____
_____
_____
_____
_____
_____

Details of the Accident

Record as much detail as possible: Direction of travel of your vehicle and the other vehicle(s), speeds, color of traffic light, road signs, statements made by other driver, statements made by witnesses, whether the other driver appeared under the influence of substances, etc.

_____
_____
_____
_____
_____
_____
_____

(use back of paper for continuation)

Appendix: Vehicle Accident Form

Use this road diagram to indicate the directions of travel and the positions of vehicles after the accident. Where appropriate, write in the names of the streets. Mark an "N" for North on the compass star as an aid to orienting the accident scene.

Questions to ask (in English and Spanish):

Please, I need some information from you. *Por favor, necesito información de usted.*
Driver's name. *Nombre del conductor*
Driver's address. *La dirección del conductor*
Driver's telephone number. *El numero de teléfono del conductor*
Driver's license information. *Información de la licencia de conductor*
    Number. *Numero*
    Issued by the state of. *De que estado es su licencia*
    Country. *De que pais es su licencia*

Owner of vehicle (from registration). *Datos del dueño del vehiculo:*
    Name. *Nombre*
    Address. *Dirección*
    Telephone number. *Numero de teléfono*
    Owner's insurance information. *Información del seguro*
    Company name. *Nombre de la compania*
    Company address. *Dirección de la compania*
    Policy number. *Numero de la poliza*
    Contact information. *Información del contacto*

Appendix: Common Conversions

Common Conversions

Measurements in Mexico are in metrics.

Outside
Temperature is measured on the Celsius scale:
- Fahrenheit = Centigrade x 1.8 + 32
- Centigrade = (Fahrenheit − 32)/1.8
- Example: 72°F = 22°C

Distance: A kilometer is shorter than a mile.
- Kilometer = .6 miles
- Mile = 1.6 kilometers
- Speed example: 40 miles/hour = 64 kilometers/hour

Inside
Oven temperature
- 325°F = 163°C
- 350°F = 177°C
- 375°F = 191°C
- 400°F = 204°C
- 425°F = 218°C
- 450°F = 232°C
- 475°F = 246°C

Weight
- Ounce = 28.4 grams
- Gram = .04 ounce
- Kilogram = 2.2 pounds
- Pound = .5 kg

Volume
- The Spanish word for teaspoon is *cucharilla,* and it's the same size.
- The Spanish word for tablespoon is *cucharada,* and it's the same size.
- The Spanish word for cup is *taza,* and it's the same size.
- A liter is a little bigger than a quart.
- Quart = .95 liter
- Liter = 1.1 quarts
- Gallon = 3.79 liters
- 20 liters (size of standard water *garrafón*) = 5.6 gallons

Length
- Inch = 2.54 centimeters
- Centimeter = .4 inch
- Foot = .3 meter
- A meter is 3 inches longer than a yard
- Yard = .9 meter
- Meter = 1.1 yard

Appendix: Telephone Dialing

Telephone Dialing

- Mexico's country code
  - 52
- Lakeside city codes
  - 387 = municipality of Jocotepec, including Jocotepec and San Juan Cosalá
  - 376 = municipality of Chapala, including Chapala and Ajijic

▶ **To call Mexico from within Mexico**
If you're using a *land-line* phone:
- To call a Mexican *land-line* phone from the same city code:
  - Only the 7-digit phone number
- To call a Mexican *land-line* phone from a different city code:
  - 01 + city code + phone #
- To call a Mexican *cell* phone:
  - 045 + city code + phone #

If you're using a *cell* phone:
- To call either a Mexican *land-line* phone or *cell* phone:
  - city code + phone #

Note: It may not be possible to call outside of Mexico using your cell phone, depending on your cell phone service plan. Therefore, the following numbers assume you are using a *land-line* phone.

▶ **To call the US or Canada from Mexico**
- 001 + area code + phone #

▶ **To call US/Canadian *toll-free numbers* from Mexico**
Use the following area codes:
- Instead of 800, dial 880
- Instead of 866, dial 883
- Instead of 877, dial 882
- Instead of 888, dial 881

Note: These will be charged at the international rate.

▶ **To call any other country from Mexico**
- 00 + country code + city code + phone #

▶ **To call Mexico from the US or Canada**
To call a Mexican *land –line* phone:
- 011 + 52 + city code + phone #

To call a Mexican *cell* phone:
- 011 + 52 + 1 + city code + phone #

Emergency Numbers and Words

Any emergency: 911
24-Hour Ambulance: **065** (Red Cross)
Red Cross **376-765-2553, or 2308**
    Hospital Ajijic **376-766-0622, or 0662**
    Clinica Maskaras **376-765-4838**
      (Riberas Del Pilar)
Clinica Municipal **376-765-5421**
  (Chapala)
Clinica Municipal **387-763-1920**
  (Jocotepec)
Police:
Police – Chapala **376-765-4444, or 2821**
Police – Ajijic **376-766-1760**
Police – Jocotepec **387-763-0006, or 0074**
Police –Movilidad **376-765-4747**
    (Chapala)
24-Hour Fire & Rescue:
For all towns **376-766-3615**
Road Service:
Green Angels **078 or 800-903-9200**
(*Los Angeles Verde*)

Common Emergency Words
Do you speak English? = *habla usted inglés?*
I don't speak Spanish = *no hablo español*
the address is = *la dirección es*
    my house = *mi casa*
I need = *necesito*
    police = *policía*
    firefighters = *bomberos*
    an ambulance = *una ambulancia*
    a doctor = *un doctor*
    there is a = *hay* (pronounced "eye") un
    man = *hombre* (om'-bre)
    woman = *mujer* (moo-herr')
    child = *niño* (boy), *niña* (girl)
    traffic accident = *accidente de tránsito*
    robber = *ladrón*
    rapist = *violador*
    fire = *incendio*
    intruder = *intruso*
    noise = *ruido*
    gun = *pistola*
    knife = *cuchillo*
    very sick = *muy enfermo*
bleeding = *hemorragia*
people are hurt = *personas son lastima*
heart attack = *ataque cardiac*
no breathing = *no respiración*
death = *muerte*
come right away, please = *venir ahorita, por favor*
hurry = *prisa*

Index

Aduana.*See* Customs (Aduana)
Ajijic19, 132, 133, 134, 138, 153, 164, 172, 173, 177, 180, 184, 185, 198, 215
Aljibe*See* Water :Cistern (Aljibe)
Apostilles - Certified Documents 71
Auctions 60, 61, 62, 63
Baking 216
Banking44, 63, 67, 68, 74, 83, 88, 117, 236, 237, 238, 239, 257
    ATM Machines21, 67, 68, 105, 117, 238
Beauty Salons and Barbers 219
Bed & Breakfast Inns19, 21, 22
Bicycles 157
Big Box Stores 185
Books 266
Border Driver30, 76, 84, 95, 100
Bribes ....*See* Mordidas
Buses30, 121, 152, 153, 154, 187
Cars ....*See* Vehicles
Chapala131, 132, 135, 136, 152
Climate 57, 124, 125, 216
CONDUSEF......................239
Conversions...............277, 278
Cooking.............................216
Credit Rating
    Mexican 238
    US 25, 44, 46

Crime15, 39, 83, 193, 194, 195, 214, 254, 256
CURP Number ...214, 237, 252
Customs (Aduana)42, 43, 56, 91, 96, 99, 119, 217
DEET 191
Dentists......................200, 201
DIF 121, 153, 200, 250, 269
Driver's License96, 120, 158, 252, 254
DVDs 56, 77, 172, 228
eBay 59, 189, 217
Electricity106, 190, 221, 222, 224
Embassy
    American................257, 268
    Canadian 257, 268
Emergency Words..............282
Expats
    Number of.......................10
Flea Markets ....*See* Tianguis
Florida 10
Fumigation – Extermination 110
Galerias Mall......................186
Garbage Collection 110, 218
Gardeners*See* Housekeepers - Gardeners
Garrafóns 175, 176, 177
Gas - Propane106, 108, 220, 221
Gasoline 88, 89, 159, 160
GPS 100
Green Angels..............101, 281
Hacienda 49
Health Care
    Cost of............114, 196, 198

283

Quality of.................15, 197
Health Insurance 69, 73, 114, 116
 IMSS 202, 203, 204, 205, 206
 Private 69, 73, 114, 206, 207
 Seguro Popular...............205
Housekeepers – Gardeners 27, 106, 117, 148, 209, 210, 211, 212
IKEA Bags...................74, 174
Immigration
 SEGOB INM..................269
INAPAM....121, 200, 250, 269
Income.....................10, 14, 36
Internet 14, 40, 76, 87, 107, 142, 225, 226, 227, 228, 229, 231, 232, 235
IPAB................................239
Jocotepec 131, 137, 138, 152, 163
Keys.....77, 106, 112, 184, 212
Lake Chapala Society 22, 110, 111, 133, 139, 143, 155, 183, 185, 187, 213, 257, 268
Language
 Instruction........69, 139, 143
 Translation Applications 75, 141
Lawyers (Abogados)..126, 127
Libel – Slander...................128
Magazines.........................266
Mail & Shipping 29, 112, 189, 216, 217
 Courier Companies..59, 218
 USPS Airmail M-Class 58, 75
Maps................100, 106, 153
Medicare.......69, 196, 203, 208
Medications 78, 83, 198, 199, 200, 205
Mordidas............120, 255, 256
Motorcycles..50, 164, 167, 168
Moving
 Companies.................53, 54
 Cost of........................34, 53
 Names.................27, 28, 92
 Negotiating Prices 147, 148, 174
Newspapers.......................266
Notario Público 23, 120, 121, 126, 158, 257
Nurseries (*viveros*).............188
Parker Insurance Agency...165
Passport 18, 25, 27, 95, 96, 99, 128, 256, 257
PayPal.......................183, 236
Pets 27, 30, 41, 43, 84, 87, 99, 111, 157, 214, 215
 Carriers...........................78
 Cats.....................42, 78, 87
 Grooming................41, 215
 Horses............................43
 International Health Certificates......79, 84, 99
 Motel 6............................87
 Quarantines...............42, 43
 Vaccinations...................79
 Veterinarians...........41, 215
Phones
 Cell 75, 77, 112, 115, 156, 162, 225, 232, 234, 238
 Land - Line 107, 225, 233
 Smart............................235
Police 40, 70, 100, 120, 127, 138, 156, 160, 161, 162, 168, 194, 254, 255, 256
Politics..............................128
PROFECO.........................191
Radio........................228, 229
Red Cross (Cruz Roja) 160, 183, 201, 202
Rental Agencies.....26, 27, 108
Rental Cars.....19, 21, 149, 150

284

Index

Renting
  Reasons for 23
RFC Number 237
S&S Auto 166
Sales Tax 50, 234
San Antonio Tlayacapan 132, 135, 153, 171, 181
San Juan Cosalá 137, 138
Social Customs 144
Social Security 14
Solar Energy 224
Spencer McMullen 127, 162, 168, 237
Tablets 225, 235
Taxis 21, 151, 152, 269
Telephone Dialing 279
Tianguis 74, 172, 173, 174
Tinaco *See* Water :Tank (Tinaco)
Tipping 21, 88, 104, 147, 151, 159, 182, 219
Tlaquepaque 187
Toll Roads (cuotas) 100
Tonalá 187
Tours 16, 154, 155, 187
TV 107, 225, 229, 231
Utilities 106, 107, 220
Vehicles
  Accident Form 270
  Accidents 70, 98, 101, 116, 127, 160, 161, 199, 201, 270
  Brokers 167
  Cost of 50
  Deposit 89, 96
  Foreign-plated 48, 49, 166, 168, 248
  Impounding 116, 127, 161, 162, 168, 169
  Insurance 49, 70, 98, 116, 150, 161, 163, 164
  License Plates 157, 158, 159, 164, 167, 168
  Nationalizing 49, 97, 165
  Permit 35, 50, 66, 91, 94, 95, 96, 98, 119, 120, 158
  Repair 162
  Selling 48, 165
  Smog Sticker 159
  Stolen 168
Visas 65, 120, 203, 240, 269
  FMM Document 35, 92, 94, 95, 96, 241, 244
  Residente Permanente 47, 48, 247
  Residente Temporal 47, 48, 242
  Travel 91
  Working Permissions 36, 184
Water 104, 105, 106, 109, 174, 175, 176, 177, 216, 220, 221, 222
  Cistern (Aljibe) 109, 221, 222
  Disinfectants 179
  Pressure 25, 109, 221, 222, 224
  Purification 25, 105, 222, 224
  Tank (Tinaco) .. 25, 109, 221
Weapons 83, 100, 129, 194

285

Made in the USA
Monee, IL
30 August 2021